BUILT FOR
SPEED
WORLD'S FASTEST ROAD CARS

pil

Publications International, Ltd.

CREDITS

We would like to thank the following vehicle owners and photographers for supplying the images in this book.

1996 McLaren; O: McLaren Automotive; P: Mirco Decet. 1998-2002 BMW: O & P: BMW Group. 1999 Shelby: O & P: Shelby American. 2001 Chevrolet: O & P: General Motors Company. 2001 Jaguar: O & P: Jaguar Land Rover Limited. 2003 Audi: O & P: Audi AG. 2003-04 Mitsubishi: O & P: Mitsubishi Motors Corporation. 2004 Roush: O & P: Roush Performance. 2004-05 Cadillac: O & P: General Motors Company. 2004-06 Pontiac: O & P: General Motors Company. 2005-11 Lotus: O & P: Group Lotus, plc. 2008-10 Audi: O & P: Audi AG. 2008-11 Tesla: O & P: Tesla, Inc. 2009 Chevrolet: O & P: General Motors Company. 2009 Nissan: O & P: Nissan Motor Co., Ltd. 2009 Pontiac: O: General Motors Company; P: Jeff Cohn. 2009-12 Cadillac: O & P: General Motors Company. 2010 Dodge: O: Fiat Chrysler Automobiles; P: Jeff Cohn. 2010 Roush: O: Roush Performance; P:Jeff Cohn. 2012 Ford: O & P: Ford Motor Company. 2014-16 Chevrolet: O & P: General Motors Company. 2014-18 BMW: O & P: BMW Group. 2015-16 Alfa Romeo: O & P: Fiat Chrysler Automobiles. 2015 Dodge: O & P: Fiat Chrysler Automobiles. 2016-17 BMW: O & P: BMW Group. 2017 Dodge: O & P: Fiat Chrysler Automobiles. 2017 Bugatti: O & P: Bugatti Motor Company. 2017-18 Chevrolet: O & P: General Motors Company. 2017 Ferrari: O & P: Ferrari Motor Company. 2017 Ford: O & P: Ford Motor Company. 2017-18 Koenigsegg: O & P: Koenigsegg Automotive AB. 2018 Aston Martin: O & P: Aston Martin Lagonda Limited. 2018 McLaren: O & P: McLaren Automotive. 2019 Chevrolet: O & P: General Motors Company. 2019 McLaren: O & P: McLaren Automotive.

Louis Weber, CEO
Publications International, Ltd.
8140 Lehigh Avenue
Morton Grove, IL 60053

Permission is never granted for commercial purposes.

ISBN: 978-1-64030-718-6

Manufactured in China.

8 7 6 5 4 3 2 1

CONTENTS

1996 MCLAREN F1 006

1998-2002 BMW Z3 M 010

1999 SHELBY SERIES 1 014

2001 CHEVROLET CORVETTE Z06 018

2001 JAGUAR XKR SILVERSTONE 022

2003 AUDI RS 6 026

2003-2004 MITSUBISHI LANCER EVOLUTION 030

2004 ROUSH MUSTANG 440A 034

2004-2005 CADILLAC XLR 038

2004-2006 PONTIAC GTO 042

2005-2011 LOTUS ELISE 046

2008-2010 AUDI S5 050

2008-2011 TESLA ROADSTER 054

2009 CHEVROLET CORVETTE ZR1 058

2009 NISSAN GT-R 062

2009 PONTIAC G8 GXP 066

2009-2012 CADILLAC CTS-V 070

2010 DODGE VIPER SRT10 074

2010 ROUSH 427R MUSTANG 078

2012 FORD MUSTANG BOSS 302 082

2014-2016 CHEVROLET SS 086

2014-2019 BMW i8 090

2015-2016 ALFA ROMEO 4C 094

2015 DODGE CHALLENGER SRT HELLCAT 098

2016-2017 BMW M2 102

2017 BUGATTI CHIRON 106

2017-2018 CHEVROLET CAMARO ZL1 110

2017 DODGE VIPER 114

2017 FERRARI LAFERRARI 118

2017 FORD GT 122

2017-2018 KOENIGSEGG AGERA RS 126

2018 ASTON MARTIN VALKYRIE 130

2018 MCLAREN 720S 134

2019 CHEVROLET CORVETTE ZR1 138

2019 MCLAREN SENNA 142

Drawing on multiple Formula 1, CanAm, and Indianapolis victories, England's McLaren organization set about creating its first road car in 1989. Revealed to the public in 1992, the McLaren F1 was on the road by 1994 and in the winner's circle at LeMans in 1995. With its no-holds-barred engineering, the F1 redefined the term "supercar." Scissor-type doors provided access to a leather interior with an unusual "1+2" layout: a form-fitting driver seat was centrally located, with a passenger seat slightly aft on both sides. A BMW-designed 6.1-liter V12 was mounted amidships and packed 627 bhp. A carbon-fiber body/chassis structure made for an unprecedented power-to-weight ratio of under four lbs per horsepower. Price and performance were equally stratospheric: $810,000, 0-60 in 3.2 seconds, 11.1-second quarter-mile times, and a 231-mph top speed. Ninety-five mph was possible in second gear. When production ceased in 1997, only 100 cars, including GTR and LeMans competition versions, had been built.

Z3 M 1998-2002

BMW unveiled its first "mass-market" two-seater with the Z3 in 1996. A "breadvan" hatchback Coupe was a model-year '99 addition. All versions borrowed running gear and chassis components from the popular 3-Series passenger-car line—hence Z3—repackaged for a trim 96.8-inch wheelbase. BMW added high-performance M versions for 1998. The M Roadster and Coupe showed considerable buffing by BMW's M (Motorsports) division, the in-house "tuner shop" that had transformed the ordinary 3-Series into the M3, one of the world's most desirable driving machines. Indeed, upgrades followed the same formula—starting with the engine, where the M3's specially built 3.2-liter inline six was the obvious choice. Initial bhp in U.S. spec was 240 versus 321 in European tune. Why the difference? Apparently, BMW felt American driving required favoring low-speed torque over high-end power, and it calibrated accordingly. The power deficit lasted only two years, as '01 U.S. Ms added a whopping 75 bhp to reach 315 total, plus a twist tweak from 236 to 251 pound-feet of torque, albeit at a zingy 4,900 rpm versus 3,800. As for acceleration, the 315-bhp cars got to 60 about a half-second ahead of 240-bhp models—4.8 versus 5.3 in *Car and Driver's* Coupe tests. Comparable M Roadsters turned in virtually identical track numbers, as both versions weigh around 3,000 pounds.

High-rate springs, shocks, and antiroll bars were expected and on hand, but the M cars also got a beefed-up rear crossmember that mounted reinforced suspension arms to carry M3 hubs. Solid ball joints were specified to link the front struts and antiroll bar for quicker steering response.

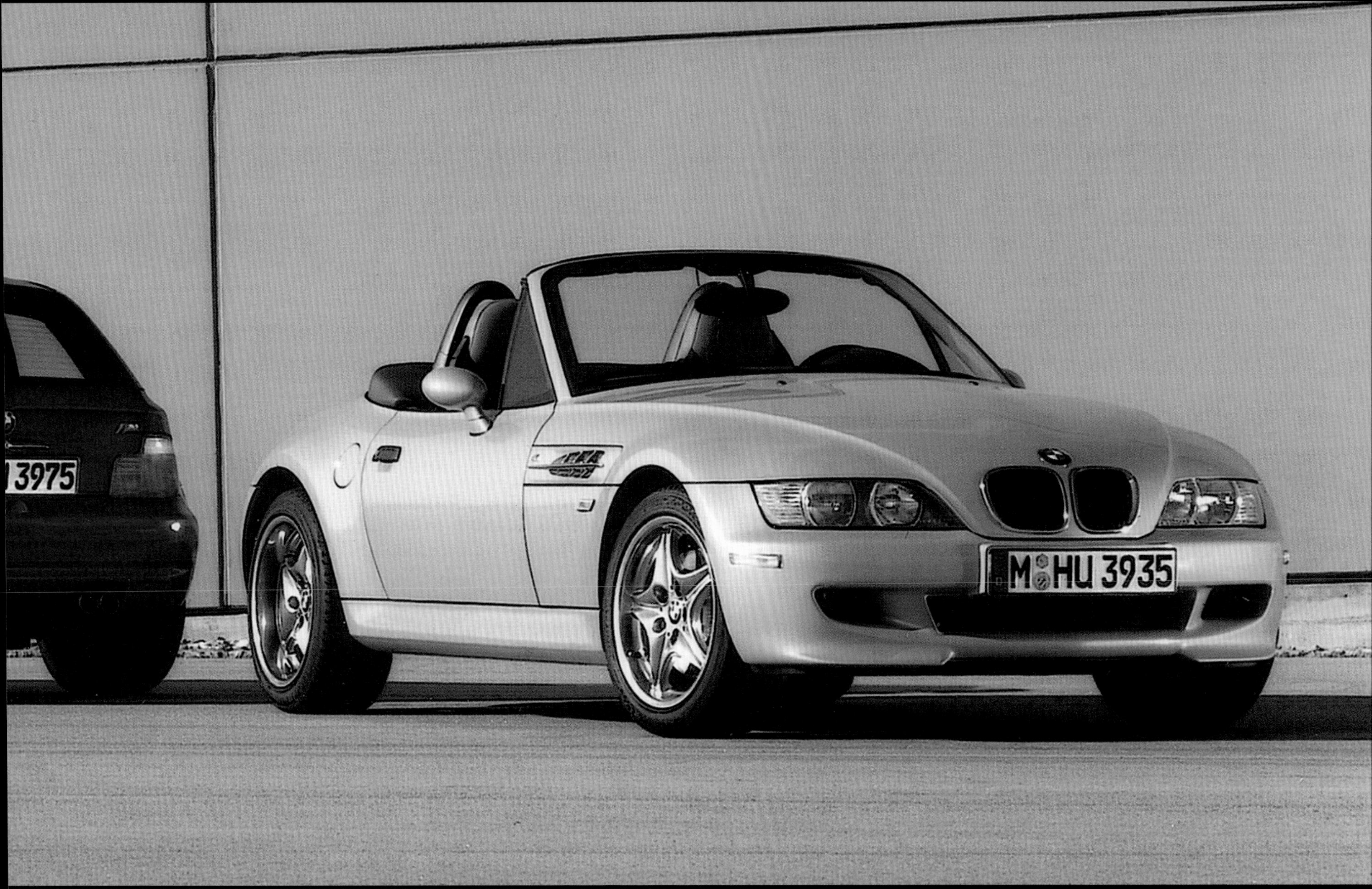
3975
M HU 3935

M-car styling differences were fairly subtle: just a quartet of exhaust pipes, a deeper front fascia (for high-speed aerodynamics), and slightly different front-fender "gills." Interior distinctions involved extra gauges down low on the center stack, more heavily bolstered seats, real-wood accents, and snazzy two-toning for "extended leather" upholstery spreading to doors, dashtop, and other surfaces.

The Coupe's fixed full-length roof also provided twice the luggage space (nine cubic feet), but resulted in love-it-or-hate-it styling. *Car and Driver* likened the look to "the unholy union of a packing crate and a gigantic sausage." Others were reminded of the old MGB GT—and hatchback Honda Civics.

Whatever faults they inherited from lesser Z3s, the Ms more than compensated for them with speed and road manners that impressed even by high BMW standards. *Road & Track's* Paul Frere greeted the Roadster as "another Munich masterpiece," praising "the enormous range of its engine. It has immediate throttle response (thanks to six separate throttle valves!) and is completely vibration free. On the road, the well-weighted steering feels accurate and responsive, and rough surfaces don't throw [the car] off its path…At the track, the M Roadster's excellent balance is fully appreciated... Nearing the limit, [the car] feels neutral, [controlled] with small corrections to the steering and throttle."

SHELBY
SERIES 1 1999

The Shelby Series 1 was Carroll Shelby's only clean-sheet design. (His other cars were modifications of designs from other manufacturers.) It was also the last hurrah from the storied Texas chicken farmer who won Le Mans, fathered the almighty Cobra, engineered Le Mans triumphs for Ford, and inspired the Viper.

The Series 1 also involved a self-styled cowboy as colorful as Carroll Shelby: Oldsmobile general manager John Rock. Rock wanted a car that would do for flagging Oldsmobile what the Shelby-influenced Viper did for Dodge, as well as a high-profile showcase for Oldsmobile's 32-valve twincam Aurora V-8. The Series 1 was no Viper, but it needed no apologies either. As Shelby himself once said: "I don't [care] how fast it'll go as long as it'll [do] somewhere about 150. . . . I'd much rather build a car that is comfortable to drive and that performs well. . . . All that Cobra stuff is passé, the old wind-in-your-face sort of thing."

The Series 1 was ten inches shorter than a Viper on an identical 96.2-inch wheelbase and was three inches wider than a C5 Corvette at 76.2. Base curb weight was 2650 pounds, fifty pounds under that of a base BMW Z3.

That helped performance, of course, but it didn't compromise the Series 1's integrity. The carbon-fiber body weighed only 130 pounds, yet was stronger than a steel shell would have been. The chassis was welded up from extruded-aluminum members. The Series 1 also had a largely aluminum suspension. At each corner were upper and lower control arms, an adjustable shock, and a coil spring attached to Formula

The aluminum control arms were C4 Corvette, but forged rather than cast, and the geometry not only minimized unsprung weight but allowed handling to be tweaked to taste. An anti-roll bar lived at each end. Claimed weight distribution was around 50/50. Steering was the predictable rack-and-pinion. Brakes, also Corvette-sourced, were hefty discs measuring 13 inches fore and 12 aft. Like early Vipers, there was no ABS.

The aluminum Aurora V-8 got new camshafts, intake manifolds, exhaust, and control chip—not wild alterations, but effective. Horsepower was 320 at 6,500 rpm, up seventy from stock, and peak torque was 290 pound-feet at 5,000, a gain of thirty. Getting the grunt to the ground was a six-speed gearbox, another Corvette item, rear-mounted in a 4.22:1 transaxle.

The Series 1 was claimed to do 0–60 mph in 4.4 seconds, 0–100 in 11 flat, and a 12.8-second quarter-mile at 109.9 mph. There was also a supercharged version that was said to do 0–60 in 3.2 seconds. Top speed was around 170 mph.

Without a major carmaker as a partner, Shelby had many hurtles and setbacks before the Series 1 reached customers. Venture Industries, supplier of the carbon-fiber body and a leading "Tier 1" vendor to Detroit stepped in with financial and technical support. Then Venture declared bankruptcy and the Series 1 was dead. Only 249 were built.

CHEVROLET
CORVETTE Z06 2001

Chevrolet Corvette gained a new Z06 performance model for 2001. The Z06 appellation was borrowed from the order code of a ready-to-race option package offered on the 1963 Corvette. The 2001 Z06 was based on Corvette's short-lived notchback-roof coupe or "hardtop" bodystyle. The hardtop was slightly lighter than the hatchback and convertible Vette's and the Z06 added weight-saving features such as a titanium exhaust system.

Powering the Z06 was an aluminum-block pushrod V-8 dubbed the LS6 (another code number resurrected from Chevy lore), based on the 346-cid LS1 engine that was first seen in the fifth-generation Corvette that debuted in 1997. Under the tomato-soup red engine covers of the LS6 was a powerplant that delivered 385 bhp at 6,000 rpm and twisted out 385 pound-feet of torque at 4,800 revs. By comparison, the standard 'Vette engine made 350 bhp at 5600 rpm and—in stickshift cars—developed 375 pound-feet of torque at 4,400 rpm.

Chevy engineers looked everywhere for ways to pack more "go" into the LS6. The intake manifold featured an enlarged plenum and more accommodating intake runners. Those deep-breathing exercises got a boost from a higher-lift steel-billet camshaft and more tightly wound valve springs. More generous fuel injectors increased flow by ten percent. The LS6's distinctively shaped pistons rose and fell under special pent-roof combustion chambers that developed a compression ratio of 10.5:1.

Chevrolet claimed the Z06 power team could reach 60 mph from a standstill in four seconds flat and run the quarter mile in 12.6 seconds at 114 mph. Consider that when the 345-horse notchback 'Vette first came out, *Road & Track* coaxed one to 0 60 mph in 5.3 seconds and ran the quarter in 13.6 ticks.

The Z06 was intended to display road-course athleticism as much as dragstrip muscle. For that, the car was given its own FE4 suspension with a heftier transverse composite leaf spring in the rear, and a hollow front stabilizer bar that was not only larger in diameter than on other Corvette suspensions, but it was made with thicker walls, too. *AutoWeek* raved about the Z06's handling after whipping over the Mid-Ohio Sports Car Course. "The steering is heavier, meatier, better. . . . [T]ouch brakes, dial in steering and the Z06 responds immediately and with conviction. . . . Set up for the 180-degree Keyhole, prepare for the front tires to howl and screech at the fight, as they had all morning in 2000-model Hardtop Corvettes, the former highest-performance version. In this Z06, even while carrying more speed, there is only mild protest."

The Z06 wasn't as purely brawny as the Dodge Viper. Nor was it as luxurious or comfortable of a grand tourer as a well-equipped Corvette hatchback and convertible. What it did, was bring enough of those qualities together in the same package at a price tag comparable to some popular sport utilities of the day. Said *Motor Trend's* Jack Keebler, "For the money, this is very likely the finest all-around all-weather two-seat sports car ever."

JAGUAR
XKR SILVERSTONE 2001

In 2001, Jaguar brought out a Silverstone edition of its grand touring XKR coupe and convertible. To XKR's equipment the Silverstone added: Platinum Silver paint, "Silverstone" writ on hood emblem and chrome door-sill plates, bird's-eye maple interior planking instead of the usual burled walnut, charcoal leather upholstery with red stitching, larger-diameter all-disc brakes by Italy's Brembo, and 20-inch wheels wearing bigger tires. The coupe chassis was further upgraded with a Performance Handling Pack comprising a slightly larger front antiroll bar, a slightly smaller rear bar, higher-rate springs, and steering with a recalibrated electronic control unit and a rack mounted on firmer bushings.

Named for the famed British airfield circuit where Jaguars raced and won, the Silverstone was an evolution of the XK-Series, which bowed as the 1997 XK8 with Jaguar's then-new 32-valve, 4.0-liter, twincam V-8 and styling with strong overtones of Jaguar's storied E-Type sports cars. The front suspension and part of the floorpan also looked to the past, being held over from the superseded XJS that dated back to 1975.

The XK8 was too heavy and luxurious to be the "sports car" Coventry said it was. But the styling implied otherwise, prompting *AutoWeek's* Pete Lyons to ask, "Is the XK8 really a neo-E? Sorry, no. . . . Then is it just a rebodied XJS? No, it's better, much better. The lively new XK8 can honestly call itself a driver's car—a fine modern GT."

Traces of XJS were in it, but the styling was drop-dead gorgeous; handling was enjoyably agile and the V-8 was a silky, whispering dynamo. But some people, including most journalists, thought the XK8 deserved more than 290 bhp. Coventry added a blown V-8 for 2000 and created the XKR, that packed 370 bhp and 387 pound-feet of torque. The supercharger made a muted, but discernible, full-throttle moan that recalled the bellow of classic prewar supercharged machines.

Despite its sporty elegance and ineffable "Olde English" Jaguar charm, the XKR proved an exhilarating ride. Most published road tests listed 0–60 mph at about 5.3 seconds regardless of body style. The standing quarter mile came up in as little as 13.7 seconds at 105 mph. Top speed was electronically limited to 156 mph, but disconnecting the governor might have increased that to 170. *Car and Driver's* test coupe generated 0.88g on the skidpad, not Corvette grippy perhaps, but impressive for a fast, smooth-riding GT weighing nearly two tons.

All these stats naturally applied to Silverstones, which weighed no more than like-equipped XKRs. Even so, the bespoke models had an edge in braking (somewhat shorter) and handling (even more adjustable). After testing one for its December 2000 issue, *Road & Track* reported "the Silverstone feels more surefooted [on the track] than the stock XKR, exhibiting less side-to-side rolling when pushed hard around tight corners. A simple lifting of the throttle will tuck the front end right back on track to the apex. And staying on the throttle a bit longer out of a corner will easily invoke a light but controllable progression of understeer to help position the car."

RS 6 2003

The 2003 Audi RS 6 was a one-and-done treat for North America—and even then squeezed out in a cluster of not quite 1,000 cars. The RS 6 was a high-performance version of Audi's midsize A6 sedan that was every bit the match for the titans from Munich, Stuttgart, and other Old World carmaking capitals. During its whirlwind tour of America, the RS 6 mightily impressed automotive writers with lightning acceleration and excellent all-wheel-drive grip—the latter a feature that set it apart from its nearest competitors.

Craft-built by Audi's performance-car subsidiary, quattro GmbH, the 6 sedan was the first RS model to make it to America. (There have subsequently been others.) The thumping heart of Audi's hot rod sedan was an enhanced version of the company's 4.2-liter aluminum V-8. With twin overhead camshafts and five valves per cylinder, it made up to 340 bhp in lesser naturally aspirated models. But with twin intercooled turbochargers and sodium-cooled exhaust valves installed, the RS 6 version delivered 450 bhp at 5,700 rpm. Torque amounted to 415 pound-feet that kicked in at a rock-bottom 1,950 rpm and stayed stout all the way to 5,600 revs. Among its closest imported power-sedan peers at the time, only the Mercedes-Benz E55 AMG could top it in these measurements.

The RS 6 possessed a powertrain that wowed critics by propelling—and that truly is the right verb—it to 0–60-mph runs of as low as 4.3 seconds, making it a near match for the E55, which had nineteen more horsepower and 101 more pound-feet of torque. Quarter mile times were in the high twelve-second zone. North America-bound models had a top speed limited at 155 mph. "The RS 6's disgorging of all its 450 horsepower is so effortless, so jetlike, that you quickly find yourself hurled into a realm where no one can hear you scream," *Automobile* said following an early test.

The suspension got a hand in doing its work from a self-adjusting system that Audi called Dynamic Ride Control. Hydraulic fluid from the shock absorbers was distributed from shock to shock. This rebalancing of fluid was designed to counteract any tendency to pitch in cornering or squat and dive in braking and accelerating. Grip from the standard quattro all-wheel drive and the 255/40ZR18 Pirelli PZero Rosso tires garnered kudos. Skidpad figures neared .9g and bested all comers in various comparison tests. However, a couple of reports mentioned palpable understeer.

All the emphasis on performance couldn't take away from the fact that the RS 6 was a luxury car, too. Standard Nappa leather sports seats were heated, as were the rear seats. The blend of qualities found within the RS 6 made it a critical hit. In a September 2003 head-to-head comparison against the E55 AMG, *Motor Trend* deemed the Audi the better car overall. Four months earlier, *Car and Driver* had ranked it the best in a field that also included the E55 AMG, the BMW M5, and the supercharged Jaguar S-type R. "[T]he RS 6's blend of power, high-speed aplomb, comfort, and superior workmanship carries the day," *C/D* said.

MITSUBISHI
LANCER EVOLUTION 2003–2004

The Mitsubishi Lancer Evolution had a rabid international fan base and a storied competition history long before most American enthusiasts had ever heard of . The Evo wouldn't arrive on our shores until 2003. Back in 1990, Mitsubishi was ungry for a World Rally Championship victory and decided that its best hopes for WRC success would lie in the compact chassis of the Lancer sedan. Engineers et about shoehorning an all-wheel drivetrain into the small Lancer platform to reate the first Evolution. To satisfy homologation rules, Mitsubishi was required to ffer street versions to the public, so the all-wheel-drive, 247-bhp Lancer Evolution debuted in Europe and Japan in 1992. All through the Nineties, ever-more-ophisticated Evolution rally cars racked up an impressive string of victories in World Rally Championship and Asia Pacific Rally Championship competition.

The 2003 Evolution was your basic, bread-and-butter Lancer sedan, only it was tuffed to the gills with high-tech performance hardware. Under the hood was Mitsu's veteran 4G63 inline four-cylinder. In the Evolution, this dohc 2.0 liter was ,ood for 271 bhp at 6,500 rpm and 273 pound-feet of torque at 3,500 rpm with he help of an intercooled twin-scroll turbo that put out a maximum 19 psi of boost.

The boxy styling of the standard Lancer never set anyone's heart afire, but the Evo's add-ons gave it a businesslike performance look and an unmistakable presence. Bulging fenders help covered 17-inch Enkei wheels on sticky Yokohama Advan P235/45ZR17 tires. Beefy Brembo brakes, complete with four-piston calipers up ront, supplied tenacious stopping power. The turbo's air-to-air intercooler was plainly visible through the thin mesh of the scowling front fascia. The hood's large vent opening expelled engine heat. An aggressive rear spoiler was perched on the decklid. Mitsubishi also offered a bare-bones Evolution RS that deleted non-race-essential equipment, along with the rear spoiler.

BUILT FOR SPEED **31**

The Evo was about no-holds-barred performance over a variety of road surfaces and in many weather conditions. Acceleration was leisurely up until about 3,500 rpm, when the turbo boost kicked in and the car rushed forward in an intoxicating, hair-raising surge. Mitsubishi's official performance figures were 0–60 in five seconds, the quarter mile in 13.9 seconds, and an estimated 155-mph top speed. These numbers were more than enough to hang with the best muscle cars of yore, and wallop any other sub-$30,000 car of its day. Plus, the Evo's go-kart-quick steering and confidence-inspiring handling made it a joy to drive quickly. The tradeoffs for the extreme cornering prowess were a stiff, occasionally punishing ride that never let you forget that you were in a tautly suspended performance car, and copious amounts of road noise from the low-profile tires.

Auto-enthusiast publications were unanimous in their praise of the Evo's sure-footed moves: "The single most impressive feature of the car is how idiot-proof it is, how easy it is to drive really fast," said *Automobile*. *Automobile* later crowned the Evo its 2004 "Automobile of the Year," going so far as to call it "very likely the automotive icon of the decade."

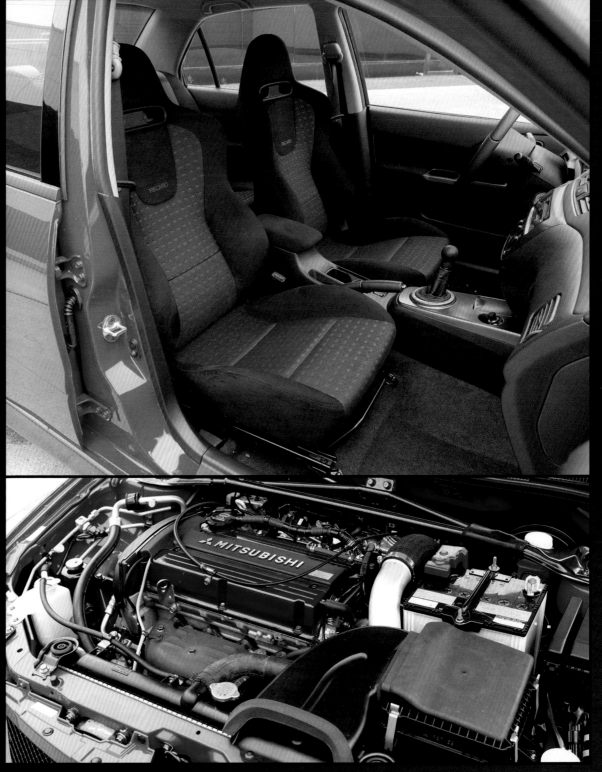

MUSTANG 440A 2004

Roush Performance, of Livonia, Michigan, was one of a handful of aftermarket firms that blossomed from bolt-on-parts supplier into car producer. Their turnkey stallions were assembled using parts from Roush's own high-performance catalog. Roush Performance had already cooked up its own hot version of the new-for-2005 Mustang, but company founder and engineering guru Jack Roush figured that the outgoing 2004 model deserved a special send-off. Hence, the limited-edition Roush 440A.

The 440A nameplate decoded like this: 400 horsepower, the 40th production year of the Mustang, and "A" for anniversary edition. The 40 also represented the production figure for the car—a mere 40 were built. Underhood, the 440A packed Ford's modular 4.6-liter V-8. This engine made 260 bhp in a stock 2004 Mustang GT, but in the 440A it cranked out 400 horsepower with the help of a Roush intercooled Roots-style supercharger.

Though the 440A retained a live rear axle and stock Mustang brakes, the chassis received a few tweaks. Roush's Stage 3 suspension setup included specially valved shocks and struts, with Roush lowering springs, dampers, aluminum rear control arms, and a 30mm front antiroll bar. Special Roush chrome five-spoke wheels mounted beefy B.F. Goodrich rubber.

Muscle Mustangs & Fast Fords magazine recorded a best ET of 13.36 seconds at 106.88 mph in a prototype 440A convertible and found the car tight and confidence-inspiring on a few road-course hot laps.

Externally, the 440A got its muscled-up look from a body kit with a unique hood, an aggressive front fascia with integrated fog lamps, rocker panel side skirts, and a rear wing. Shelbyesque racing stripes covered the hood, roof, rocker panels, and decklid.

Sticker prices ranged from $51,000 to $58,000, depending on equipment. In both physical modifications and overall spirit, Roush's Mustangs were considered successors to Carroll Shelby's legendary GT-350s and GT-500s. Jack Roush might not have been quite the household name among enthusiasts that Carroll Shelby was, but his career was no less impressive. Roush had 40 years of hands-on experience with Ford products, and an amazing record of wins in a wide range of competition, from drag racing, to road racing, to NASCAR.

For a large number of enthusiasts who lusted after Detroit's big-block bad boys of the late Sixties and early Seventies, cars like the 440A offered the best of both worlds. They were refined, with more modern build quality and ergonomics, along with safety features such as airbags and four-wheel disc brakes—but they weren't too refined. They were just rough enough around the edges to remind their baby-boomer drivers what it used to be like in the good ol' days, before there were newfangled turbochargers, intercooler sprayers, and driver-programmable all-wheel-drive systems.

A Roush 440A could honestly plant you back in your seat the old-fashioned way: with American V-8 horsepower.

The Cadillac XLR that debuted in 2004 was a suave Mercedes SL fighter based on Chevrolet Corvette bones. Yet the XLR looked nothing like a Corvette or the SL, had a pure Cadillac heart, and was plenty fast. The XLR was basically the for-sale version of the 1999 Evoq concept car, the first public hint that Cadillac's future in the 21st century would not be like Cadillac's past. At the time the Evoq broke cover, General Motors's luxury brand was some two years into a $4 billion extreme makeover dubbed "Art & Science."

The XLR was not a Corvette in a Cadillac suit, though the similarities were undeniable. For starters, both had front-mounted V-8s, rear transaxles, and composite-paneled bodies. Apart from looks and intended audience, it was the powertrain that most separated the GM twosome. The C6 Corvette, of course, boasted Chevy's 6.0-liter LS2 ohv V-8 with a stout 400 bhp. The XLR predictably used Cadillac's own dual-cam 4.6-liter Northstar V-8, only it was a reengineered "Gen II" version developed for rear- and all-wheel-drive models vs. the original Northstar's strictly front-drive applications. Highlights included continuously variable cam timing for both intake and exhaust valves, new cylinder heads with freer-flow ports and higher compression (10.5:1), stiffer block and crank, low-friction polymer-coated pistons, manifolds redesigned for quieter running, and "by-wire" electronic throttle control. The result of all this was 320 bhp at a zingy 6,400 rpm, and 310 pound-feet of torque at 4,400.

Another distinction was the XLR's mandatory five-speed automatic transmission with manual shift gate vs. Corvette's four-speed automatic or six-speed manual. The XLR also replaced the 'Vette's conventional convertible top with a disappearing hardtop and added luxury-class equipment.

Most every road test at the time judged the XLR one "Xcellent Luxury Roadster." Indeed, the critics praised most everything about it, from the smooth, quiet acceleration—0–60 mph took no more than the factory-claimed 5.9 seconds—to satisfying backroad agility, controlled but comfortable ride, and terrific build quality. Cadillac worked extra hard on that last one, setting up a separate XLR assembly operation that shared only the Bowling Green paint shop and chassis-welding area with Corvette.

There were two bones of contention, though. The power steering still left something to be desired for precision and feedback, and some deemed the run-flat Michelins a bit narrow and soft-sidewalled for best handling. Then again, the XLR hardly wanted for skidpad grip—*Car and Driver* reported 0.83g, *Road & Track* a fine 0.88. A Mercedes SL500 had more cornering power, but was slower in a straight line and cost some $11,000 more.

In all, the XLR was arguably the most impressive new Cadillac since the '67 Eldorado. "[T]here is no question that [it's] a strong entry in the prestigious roadster class," concluded *C/D's* Csaba Csere. "Cadillac's march toward luxury credibility has reached another important milestone."

40 CADILLAC XLR 2004–2005

The 2004-06 Pontiac GTO shared nothing with the hallowed Goats of yore aside from rear-wheel drive and a thumping V-8. That's because it was an Americanized version of the four-seat Holden Monaro coupe from GM's Australian branch. Bob Lutz, celebrated GM vice-chairman and "product czar," looked hard at the Monaro in early 2002 as a sales- and image-booster for the struggling Pontiac brand—a timely idea with the Firebird ponycar then on the way out. Lutz liked what he saw and soon confirmed the Monaro would come stateside for 2004 as the first GTO in 30 years.

Though it seemed like just a Monaro with a twin-port Pontiac grille and left-hand drive, *Road & Track* noted 475 unique parts, "about 20 percent of the car."

The GTO was rather large for a modern midsize. Curb weight was a burly 3770 pounds, but that was no strain for a 5.7-liter/350-cid LS1 V-8 lifted more or less intact from the base C5 Corvette. With 350 bhp and 365 pound-feet of torque on 10.1:1 compression, the Yank outmuscled its Aussie cousin by about 50 horses and 25 pound-feet. Mr. Lutz didn't fool around. A four-speed automatic transmission was standard; $695 bought a sturdy Tremec T56 six-speed manual.

Acceleration was predictably vivid. *Road & Track's* manual-equipped '04 clocked 0-60 mph in 5.3 seconds, 0-100 in 12.9, and a standing quarter-mile of 13.8 seconds at 103.8 mph, stats to shut down the fastest showroom Goats of the golden age. Yet this was no cart-sprung, limp-wristed rocket that fell to pieces on twisty roads. The new GTO provided assured Euro-style handling with little cornering lean, fine grip—0.81g on the *R&T* skidpad—and clear, properly weighted steering, plus braking finesse and mechanical refinement classic GTOs never knew. In fact, this car drove like a posh big BMW coupe playing a Sixties-style Motown soundtrack.

Which was precisely the trouble. For aging Goat lovers and many younger critics, this reincarnation, however rapid and tuneful, was just too civilized to be a real GTO. The reborn GTO was quite the high-performance bargain, but sales were sluggish. Sensibly, Pontiac scaled back production for 2005 and added not one hood scoop but two. They didn't connect to a power-boosting Ram-Air setup, but they did help cool a more muscular V-8: the new 6.0-liter/364-cid LS2 from the C6 Corvette. Outputs jumped to 400 bhp and 395 pound-feet. A scoopless hood continued as a no-cost option. The 2006 edition got only a few cosmetic tweaks and optional 18-inch wheels. Base price had hardly budged, but demand remained stagnant. With conserving cash now imperative for GM, the GTO was cancelled after the '06 run.

It's a shame the Aussie Goat left so soon. Said *Car and Driver*, "[A]s the song goes, you won't know what you've got till it's gone."

Lotus cofounder Colin Chapman said, "Adding power makes you faster on the straights, subtracting weight makes you faster everywhere". More than a decade after Chapman's 1982 death, his successors proved they still believed in weight reduction with the flyweight Elise, launched in Europe in 1996. Destined to become the best-selling Lotus ever, the Elise took a few more years to jump the pond to the U.S., but it was worth the wait for drivers who appreciated racer-sharp handling and a high level of car/driver symbiosis.

The mid-engine two-seater tipped the scales at around 1,600 pounds at the time of its debut. When it finally went on sale in the U.S. in mid 2004 as an '05 model, it was as a more crashworthy "Series 2" version that had bulked up, but only in the vicinity of 1,950 pounds.

The American Elise was powered by a Toyota 1.8-liter four-cylinder engine from the Celica GT-S that Lotus tuned to produce 190 bhp at 7,800 rpm and 138 pound-feet of torque at 6,800 revs. That output gave it a fairly low power-to-weight ratio of just over 10 pounds per horsepower. The gearbox was the same six-speed manual found in the GT-S.

The enthusiast press in the U.S. was smitten with the federalized Elise from the first. Glowing reviews especially praised its responsive steering, sticky grip, and nearly understeer-free manners. (*Motor Trend* and *Automobile* both invoked images of go-karts.) *Motor Trend* concluded, "The Elise is, by most reasonable measures, the best-handling car you can buy today."

The engine got plenty of love, too. "As revs climb and the VVTL-i kicks in, the Elise reacts with an immediate burst of energy accompanied by a more vocal response from the intake and exhaust," noted *Road & Track*. Lotus estimated a 4.9-second 0–60-mph time, but a couple of testers were a few tenths quicker. Quarter mile times were in the low-thirteen-second range.

For 2008, a supercharged SC version joined the naturally-aspirated engine. The SC engine was the same modified Toyota four, but with a Magnuson-built Roots-type blower that raised output to 218 bhp at 8,000 rpm and torque to 156 pound-feet at 5,000 rpm—and more than compensated for the fact that the car now weighed 2,006 pounds. Standing-start sprints to 60 mph took about 4.5 seconds, but 13.3 seconds in the quarter mile wasn't any better than the unblown car had gotten a few years earlier.

Styling was tweaked for 2011 and that was the end of the Elise story in the U.S. For one thing, Toyota stopped making the engine. Plus, Lotus's waiver for selling cars in the U.S. without "smart" air bags was destined to expire that summer. Certifying a new engine and doing the engineering necessary to meet the air bag standard was too much for what was essentially a limited-edition car.

While gone from America, Elise was still on sale in markets around the world. An exit from the U.S. market didn't diminish the intrinsic value of the Elise as it was during its years in America. Thrilling driving was thrilling driving—as the car's relative popularity proved.

Road & Track called the Audi S5 a "hard-charging, road-gripping German tourer of the first order." The S5 went on sale in late 2007 and inaugurated the high-style A5/S5 series that slotted between the compact A4 and midsize A6 groupings. The S5 was the high-performance version of the A5 coupe.

The S5 and A5 were Audi's first sports coupes in twenty years, spiritual successors to the five-cylinder front-drive GT and turbocharged Quattro fastbacks of 1981-91. That first square-rigged Quattro marked the Audi brand's coming of age, winning two drivers' and manufacturers' titles in international rallying and touching off a short-lived craze in AWD road cars that later blossomed anew, particularly among premium brands.

S5 coupes were motivated exclusively by Audi's familiar all-aluminum 4.2-liter (254-cid) twincam V-8 with four variably timed valves per cylinder. In that application it delivered 354 bhp right at redline, 7,000 rpm, and a healthy 325 pound-feet of torque at 3,500, aided by a high 11.0:1 compression ratio made possible by direct fuel injection. Transmission choices involved a six-speed manual or ZF's six-speed Tiptronic torque-converter automatic with manual shift gate and steering-wheel paddles.

The S5's styling was crafted by Italian-born Walter de Silva, who came to Audi after a stint at Alfa Romeo. It was a handsome coupe: chunky, muscular, and well-proportioned, with adept surface development and well-managed reflections. It would have looked even better without B-posts, but that would have required weighty structural reinforcements and the S5 already scaled a hefty 3,795 pounds at the curb. (Quattro got part of the blame, as usual.) One nifty touch was the row of LED running lamps curling beneath each headlamp module like Black Bart's mustache.

The S5 was about the same size as a BMW 3-Series two-door and Mercedes-Benz E-Class coupe, standing 182.5 inches long, 73 inches wide, and 53.9 inches high over a 108.3-inch wheelbase. Like most coupes, it was a cozy 2+2, not a practical five-seater. A full-length center console eliminated the rear center position anyway. This relative lack of total passenger space was somewhat offset by Audi's standard-setting cabin execution. That meant the S5 was as lovely inside as it was outside, with scads of aromatic leather and tasteful dollops of aluminum that could be replaced by optional wood, stainless-steel, or carbon-fiber accents.

For all its heft and luxury, the S5 claimed impressive performance stats. Most road tests reported 0–60 mph in a quick 4.8 seconds or so (with manual), standing quarter mile runs in about 13 seconds at 105 mph, and more than 0.90g of skidpad grip. What these numbers didn't convey was the smooth sophistication with which the S5 got about its business.

The Audi S5 coupe was one of the most refined, capable, and satisfying 2+2s of its time, not to mention one of the prettiest. *Road & Track* rightly called it "a treat for all the senses."

ROADSTER 2008–2011

The 2008 Tesla Roadster was the first modern, dedicated, highway-speed, production electric car sold in this country. (GM's EV-1 was only leased). Today, Tesla is selling sedans and SUVs, but the company's first product was a small sports car. The low-production Roadster allowed Tesla to test its cutting-edge engineering before rolling out its higher-volume models.

Tesla is a California-based company cofounded by Elon Musk, a man of big dollars and even bigger dreams who made the bulk of his multibillions through the sale of PayPal in 2002. Early prototypes of the Roadster were displayed in the second half of 2006, with the first production model going to Musk himself in March 2008. It's unclear whether Musk paid the full $109,000 list price (minus a $7,500 tax credit) or got an employee discount.

The Roadster's sleek carbon-fiber body was made in France, then shipped to Lotus of England for placement on a specially designed chassis. Although the outcome looked much like a stretched Lotus Elise, Tesla said only about six percent of the parts were shared between the two cars. After assembly, the body/chassis was shipped to Tesla's shop in Menlo Park, California, to have the battery pack (6,831 lithium-ion laptop-computer batteries), powertrain, and electronic controller installed.

The first Roadsters had a 248-horsepower motor. By 2010, horsepower had been increased to 288. Furthermore, a Sport edition was added that had the same 288 bhp but more torque (295 pound-feet versus 273) that dropped the 0–60 time to 3.7 seconds—a figure matched by only a handful of cars, all of which relied on boatloads of gasoline to achieve the desired results. Acceleration was explosive and instantaneous at any speed. There was only one gear, so there was never a wait for the transmission to downshift. Touch the throttle and the Tesla jumped; nail it and it pinned you to your seat. There was little body lean in corners, and the Tesla exhibited seriously sporty moves. Steering was tight and go-kart quick. The Roadster wasn't without faults. The steering, being unassisted, was quite heavy at parking and even around-town speeds. Ingress and egress were cumbersome at best. Once inside, it was a snug fit for two, as adults—even not-particularly wide ones—sat shoulder-to-shoulder. Also, while visibility to the front and sides was fine, there was but a tunnel-vision image in the rearview mirror, and the lengthy rear roof pillars obstructed nearly everything over your shoulders.

For 2011, Tesla introduced the Roadster 2.5, the most noticeable change was a revised front fascia. But the cars also got a new rear diffuser, restyled wheels, more supportive seats, additional sound insulation, and an optional seven-inch touchscreen display with backup camera that helped backing up.

Perhaps the Tesla Roadster's most profound contribution to automotive history was that it was the first such car to so vividly demonstrate the promise of electric vehicles. The fact that it was staggeringly quick, a thrill to drive, and possibly the ultimate automotive conversation piece was only icing on the cake.

CORVETTE ZR1 2009

The Chevrolet Corvette ZR1 was back for 2009 packing a V-8 with 638 bhp and 604 pound-feet of torque. It was capable of 0–60 mph in less than 3.5 seconds, and had a top speed around 200 mph. All that was wrapped in a package that was docile enough to be usable as a daily driver and that the EPA said would get twenty mpg on the highway. The ZR1 name first appeared in Corvette lore as a high-performance engine option on 1970–72 models. The ZR-1 (with a hyphen) designation was revived in 1990–95 for the fastest version of the Corvette during those years.

The 2009 ZR1 started with the aluminum frame of the high-performance Corvette Z06. To it, GM added lightweight, yet incredibly strong, carbon fiber. The hood, front fenders, roof panel, roof bow, front fascia splitter, and rocker models were all made of the stuff. A fully assembled ZR1 tipped the scale at just 3,324 pounds.

The ZR1 was light on its feet. All ZR1s came with a specially tuned version of GM's Magnetic Selective Ride Control, which used sensors to automatically adjust suspension damping to suit road conditions. *Consumer Guide®* opined, "[It's no] luxury sedan, but the ZR1's ride control is quite good for a vehicle that emphasizes acceleration and handling. One of Chevy's goals in designing this super Corvette was to make it livable as a daily driver. By and large, the company's efforts were successful. It still bangs and crashes over large pavement breaks, but it absorbs bumps as well as can be expected."

The 2009 ZR1 used a variant of the C6 Corvette's 6.2-liter ohv V-8. Unlike other supercars, the ZR1 had pushrod-activated valves instead of the usual multiple overhead cams. Dubbed "LS9" in GM-speak, the ZR1 produced 638 bhp courtesy of an Eaton supercharger—more than any production Corvette up to that date. A polycarbonate window set in the hood provided a view of the supercharger's intercooler, just in case overwhelming thrust wasn't enough to remind you that something truly special was under the hood.

Putting that much power to pavement required a special transmission. ZR1 packed a Tremec six-speed manual with a dual-disc clutch that more effectively distributed torque than a single-disc setup. It also provided for much smoother pedal action that made the car actually easy to negotiate in heavy traffic.

Straight-line performance numbers were sure to impress even the most jaded gearhead. *Motor Trend* ripped a 0–60 sprint in 3.3 seconds, with a quarter-mile run of 11.2 seconds at 130.5 mph. When the track turned twisty, the mag recorded lateral grip of 1.10g. Against the Ferrari 599 GTB Fiorano with which *MT* compared the ZR1, the prancing horse managed "just" 0.95g. Said the *MT* editors, "Performance-wise, the ZR1 trumps the 599 GTB in almost every objective category. It's also about one-third the Ferrari's price. Which is to say, Chevy's newest Vette has earned a rightful, exalted spot in the Pantheon of supercars."

NISSAN
GT-R 2009

It might have been the most famous Nissan that you'd never heard of—unless you kept up with international automotive unobtainium, followed the drifting crowd, or exercised your inner Andretti at the virtual controls of your Sony PlayStation. But the GT-R had long been worshiped by the automotive underground even outside its home market of Japan, the only country in which it was officially sold—until 2009.

The GT-R traced its history back to the late Sixties. GT-Rs held numerous records at the Pikes Peak Hillclimb and on Germany's Nürburgring. They were also terrors on the street, establishing a performance legacy that lived on—and extended well beyond Japan's borders. There were several gaps in the GT-R lineage with the last ending with the debut of the fifth generation GT-R in the fall of 2008. That GT-R had a 3.8-liter twin-turbo V-6 rated at 480 bhp at 6400 rpm and 430 pound-feet of torque starting at 3,200 rpm. Some believed those figures were understated with actual horsepower in 500 to 575 range and torque closer to 490 pound-feet. Transmitting the power was a rear-mounted six-speed "automated manual" dual-clutch transaxle with paddle shifters, and a sophisticated all-wheel-drive system.

The Nissan GT-R might well have been the performance deal of its day. Consider these numbers: 3.4, 11.8, 193, and $72,880. Those were the 0–60-mph time, quarter-mile ET, top speed, and as-tested price of a GT-R thrashed by *Road & Track*. Other buff books had posted similar performance figures. It was impossible to have duplicated the first three at anywhere close to the fourth.

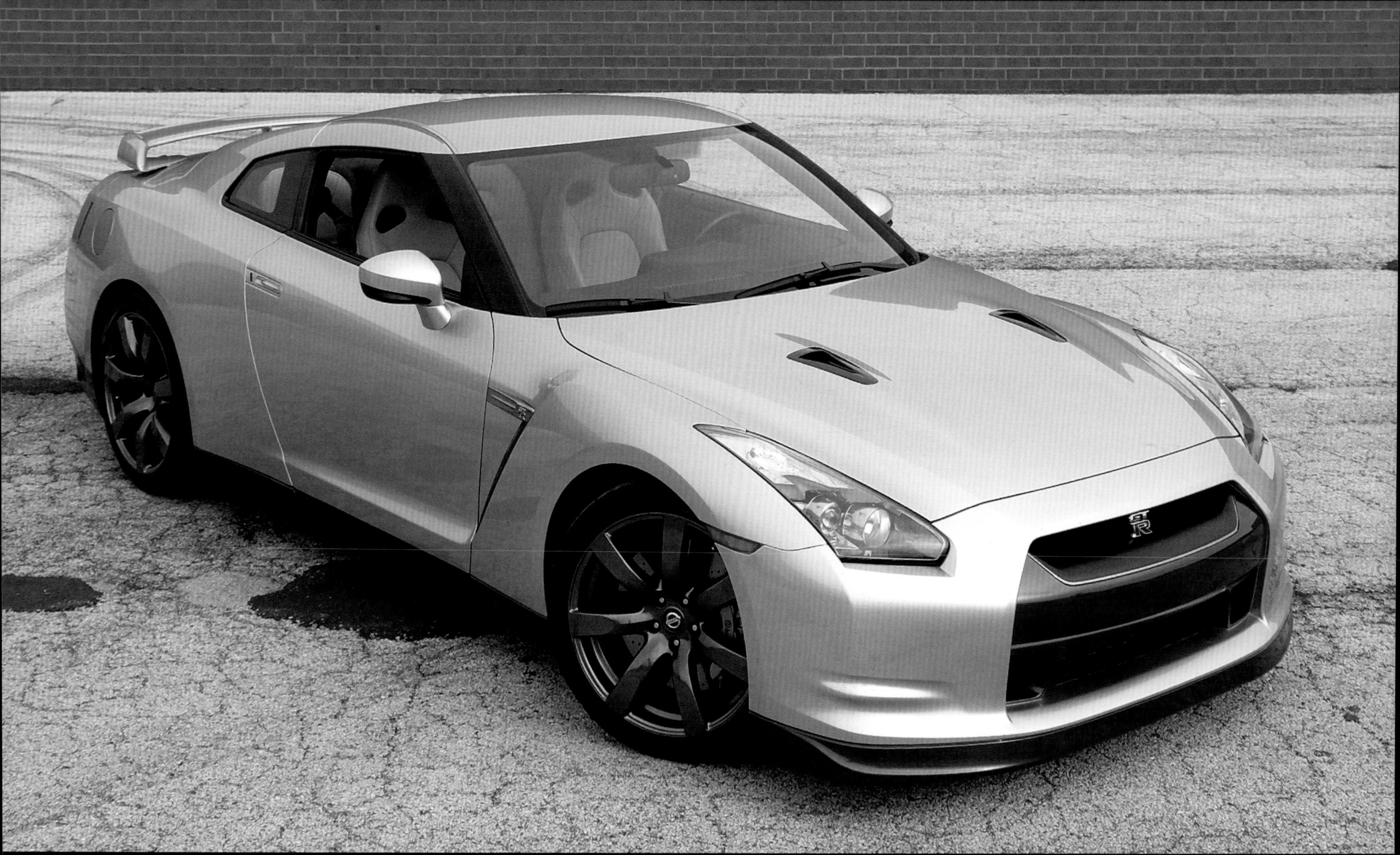

One reason for those impressive acceleration numbers was Launch Control. Launch Control worked something like this: Choose the "R" (Race) setting for the transmission and suspension, and switch off the stability control. Select the transmission's manual-shift mode with the gear lever. Hold down the brake pedal while flooring the gas. The engine would rev to about 4,500 rpm, hold there, and when you sidestepped the brake, the car launched "like an arrow from a crossbow," according to *Motor Trend*. The AWD system got at least partial credit, as it momentarily sent some power to the front wheels for better bite off the line. Thereafter, the transmission's quick shifts—which needed to be done manually via the steering-wheel paddles and came up very quickly—resulted in virtually zero power slack until you lifted off the loud pedal.

Although it was a boon to acceleration times, the transmission wasn't exactly a paragon of smoothness. When coming to a stop, the trans jolted down one gear at a time and occasionally jerked on gentle takeoffs, that made stop-and-go driving a head-wobbling affair. It was a similar story out on the highway. Floor the throttle and you could count as the transmission dropped down one gear at a time to the desired ratio. And a "countdown" it was; when the proper gear was finally summoned, the car exploded into warp drive that had you reaching "Good morning, judge" speeds in very short order.

G8 GXP 2009

Pontiac went down with flags flying and guns blazing. The Pontiac G8's performance actually exceeded that of cars from Poncho's glorious muscle car years. Built in Australia and based on the Commodore VE by Holden, General Motors's branch "down under," G8 was Pontiac's first large rear-drive sedan since the Parisienne was retired in 1986. But it was also the last widely acclaimed product from Pontiac, a car barely able to get grounded in the market before a financially battered GM pulled the plug on its parent division in 2009.

The G8 wasn't able to save Pontiac, but that shouldn't reduce the car's reputation. It was hailed by enthusiasts and well received by the automotive press. G8 arrived as a 2008 model in base form with a 256-horsepower 3.6-liter V-6 and as a GT with a 361-bhp 6.0-liter V-8. The high-performance GXP variant arrived for 2009. While most of these Aussie-built Pontiacs were powered by burly V-8s, the G8 GXP of 2009 stood out as king of this hill. The G8 GXP packed a slightly detuned Corvette engine under its hood. The 6.2-liter LS3 was rated at 415 bhp and 415 pound-feet of torque—down only 15 ponies from the Corvette original. A six-speed automatic was standard. GXP was the only G8 available with a six-speed manual transmission.

Pontiac cited the GXP's 0–60-mph time at 4.7 seconds, with a quarter mile time of 13 seconds flat at 108 mph. GXP performance came at a price at the gas pump. EPA-estimated fuel economy was thirteen mpg city/twenty highway, numbers that earned GXP a $1,700 gas-guzzler tax.

All G8s used four-wheel independent suspension, but the GXP's was tuned at Germany's famed Nürburgring race circuit. The rubber was 245/40R19 Bridgestone Potenza RE050As mounted on polished-aluminum wheels. *Automobile* magazine said this resulted in one of the most neutral-handling sedans on the market. Stopping power was upgraded from the standard G8 setup as well. Brembo four-piston calipers grabbed 14-inch rotors in front; in the back, single-piston calipers worked on 12.76-inch rotors.

GXP's base price was just more than $40,000 including the destination charge and the gas-guzzler tax. This was a nearly $8,000 premium over the already muscular and very capable G8 GT, but the pricing was pretty competitive with Dodge's burly Hemi-powered Charger SRT8.

Following the announcement of Pontiac's imminent closing in late April 2009, G8 production was quickly halted. According to sources at GM, a total of 26,368 2009 Pontiac G8s were produced. Of those, only 1,824 were the top-dog GXP model. Of them, 981 were fitted with the automatic transmission and 843 were built with the six-speed manual. The short-lived Pontiac G8 GXP deserved a spot on lists of the best high-performance Pontiacs of all time. The fact that this very special sedan came at the tail end of the brand's existence—and in very low production numbers—only made the GXP more desirable.

CTS-V 2009–2012

Cadillac's second-generation CTS-V debuted for '09 packing the most-powerful production engine that Cadillac had ever offered: a revised Chevrolet Corvette ZR1 supercharged and intercooled LS9 6.2-liter V-8. The Cadillac variant, dubbed LSA, received unique tuning and components aimed at increasing quietness and refinement, but with little performance sacrifice.

The numbers were jaw-dropping: 556 horsepower at 6,100 rpm, and 551 pound-feet of torque at 3,800 rpm. For comparison, the 2009 Mercedes-Benz E63 AMG was rated at 507 bhp, the '09 BMW M5 at 500 bhp. If the original CTS-V was Cadillac stomping on its velour-interior/vinyl-top/wire-wheel-cover/V-8-6-4 past, then the second-gen CTS-V was an emphatic grinding of the boot heel.

CTS-V offered a choice of transmissions: a Tremec TR-6060 six-speed manual or General Motors' Hydramatic 6L90-E six-speed automatic with steering-wheel-mounted buttons for manual shifting.

A handful of performance-themed design alterations differentiated the V from its regular-line CTS siblings. All these changes added a just-right dollop of ominousness to the CTS's already aggressive shape.

Cadillac claimed the CTS-V could accelerate from 0–60 mph in 3.9 seconds and do the quarter mile in twelve seconds at 118 mph, but magazine road testers generally couldn't replicate those numbers. Most road tests returned 0–60 times in the low-to-mid fours and quarter miles in the low-to-mid twelves—still world-class. Cadillac engineers aimed for a "bimodal nature" with the CTS-V, so the near-supernatural performance capabilities didn't seriously compromise the luxury and refinement expected of a premium-brand sedan. Outside of a noticeably stiffer ride and a menacing exhaust note, the CTS-V gave up little to its tamer siblings in mundane stop-and-go driving.

Cadillac was eager to prove the CTS-V's supercar bona fides beyond the expected routine of buff-book road tests and "shootouts." In May 2008, GM Performance Division executive John Heinricy piloted a stock automatic-transmission '09 CTS-V to a blistering 7:59.32 lap of Germany's famed Nürburgring Nordschleife road-race course. Cadillac claimed this was the first sub-eight-minute lap of the 'Ring recorded by a production performance sedan on street tires.

For 2011, a slick coupe and station wagon joined the CTS-V sedan. The coupe and wagon were mechanically identical to the sedan but possessed the obvious benefits and drawbacks of their respective body configurations. Compared to the sedan, both had slightly compromised rear visibility. The wagon came standard with a power liftgate and nearly doubled the sedan's carrying capacity, with twenty-five cubic feet of cargo space behind the rear seats. With the rear seats folded, that number grew to 53.4 cubic feet.

Regardless of body style, the second-gen CTS-V's "Standard of the World" levels of performance went a long way toward erasing memories of some embarrassing Cadillacs from the then, not-too-distant past.

VIPER SRT10 2010

The 2010 Dodge Viper SRT10 closed out Viper's second generation. All Vipers had a preference for function over comfort. That was true of the second-generation Viper, which was introduced for 2003 and updated in 2008 with improvements that served it through 2010. Its V-10 engine displaced 8.4 liters (510 cubic inches) and put out 600 bhp and 560 pound-feet of torque. The V-10 had an aluminum block and pushrod-operated overhead valves. Overhead-valve gear seemed more like a Sixties muscle car spec not twenty-first-century modern high tech, but the Viper had variable valve timing for optimum power at all engine speeds. The cars used heavy-duty components such as forged powder-metal connecting rods secured with aircraft-quality fasteners—which gave an instant leg up to Vipers that were bought by people who intended to race them. The engine also looked great. In age when performance-car engines were shrouded with plastic, Viper had long metal valve covers painted in a red crackle finish clearly on display whenever the hood was raised.

With its 600-bhp engine and approximately 3,500-pound curb weight, Viper could do 0–60 mph in less than four seconds and the quarter-mile in the low-twelve-second range. Top speed was around 200 mph. Vipers could stop well too. Dodge claimed the Brembo brakes with big 14-inch rotors could halt a Viper in less than 100 feet from 60 mph (though period tests by *Road & Track* reported stops in the 112- to 116-foot range) and the car could accelerate and brake 0–100–0 in just 11 seconds. The four-wheel independent suspension used aluminum control arms. Big 275/35ZR18 front and 345/30ZR19 rear tires ensured impressive grip in turns.

The price for the '10 Viper SRT10 roadster was $90,255, while the coupe cost $91,005. Thanks in part to Dodge's emphasis on power over creature comforts and high-tech wizardry, the Viper was always a performance bargain—at least by supercar standards.

Road & Track's Peter Egan captured the Viper driving experience well in an article entitled "The 600-Horsepower Club." (The Bentley Continental GT Speed, Chevrolet Corvette ZR1, Ferrari 599 GTB Fiorano, Lamborghini Merciélago LP640, Mercedes-Benz SL65 AMG, and the Viper constituted this elite fraternity.) "An ideal cross-country GT car it's not, but on the twisty back roads it works pretty well," said Egan. "Grip is excellent—if a little busy over mid-corner bumps—and the balance is good. Steering kickback is less filtered than with the other cars, but there's a satisfying sense of driving the car with your own seat-of-the-pants instincts. It'll generate over 1.0g of grip on the skidpad and get through the slalom almost as fast as the Ferrari 599, so you've got plenty of traction to work with. And tons of power from the naturally aspirated ohv V-10—unique in this group. Its sub-100-grand price tag is also unique."

Dodge Viper was an American original. Carroll Shelby had a hand in the original Viper's development. Just as the Shelby's Cobra 427 was brutally fast, often hard to handle, and uncomfortable, so was the Viper. True Viper devotees ignored the discomfort and took pleasure in mastering the power.

Every Roush Mustang 427R started life with good bones, those of the Ford Mustang. Plucked from the assembly line at the peak of freshness, lucky Mustang GTs were selected from the queue destined for dealerships and redirected to Roush Performance in Livonia, Michigan.

Founded by racing jack-of-all-trades and one-time Ford engineer Jack Roush, Roush Performance has been modifying Mustangs since 1998. A 2010 *Consumer Guide®* Automotive Best Buy, the stock Mustang GT was already a fine ride. In the hands of Roush Performance, those cars were morphed in a manner akin to Pinocchio's conversion from wooden puppet to real boy.

And like Pinocchio, the 427R had a good heart. Already beating strongly in the stock Mustang GT, the 4.6-liter three-valve V-8 was boosted by a healthy 120 bhp compliments of Roush Charging. A supercharger designed and built in-house by Roush, the intercooled Roush Charger, along with a few other tweaks, raised peak engine output to 435 bhp and a stout 400 pound-feet or torque. An upgraded cooling system was also part of the deal.

Predictably, there was more to the 427R package than just power. To help this puppet-turned-boy learn to walk without strings, Roush thoroughly worked over the suspension, and replaced the front and rear springs, struts, and sway bars with equipment from the Roush Performance Catalog. Specific wheels and tires were also included.

Also part of the package were cabin and body-trim enhancements too numerous to list here. Understandably proud of its creation, Roush took care to apply its name to the vehicle more times than we could have accurately counted.

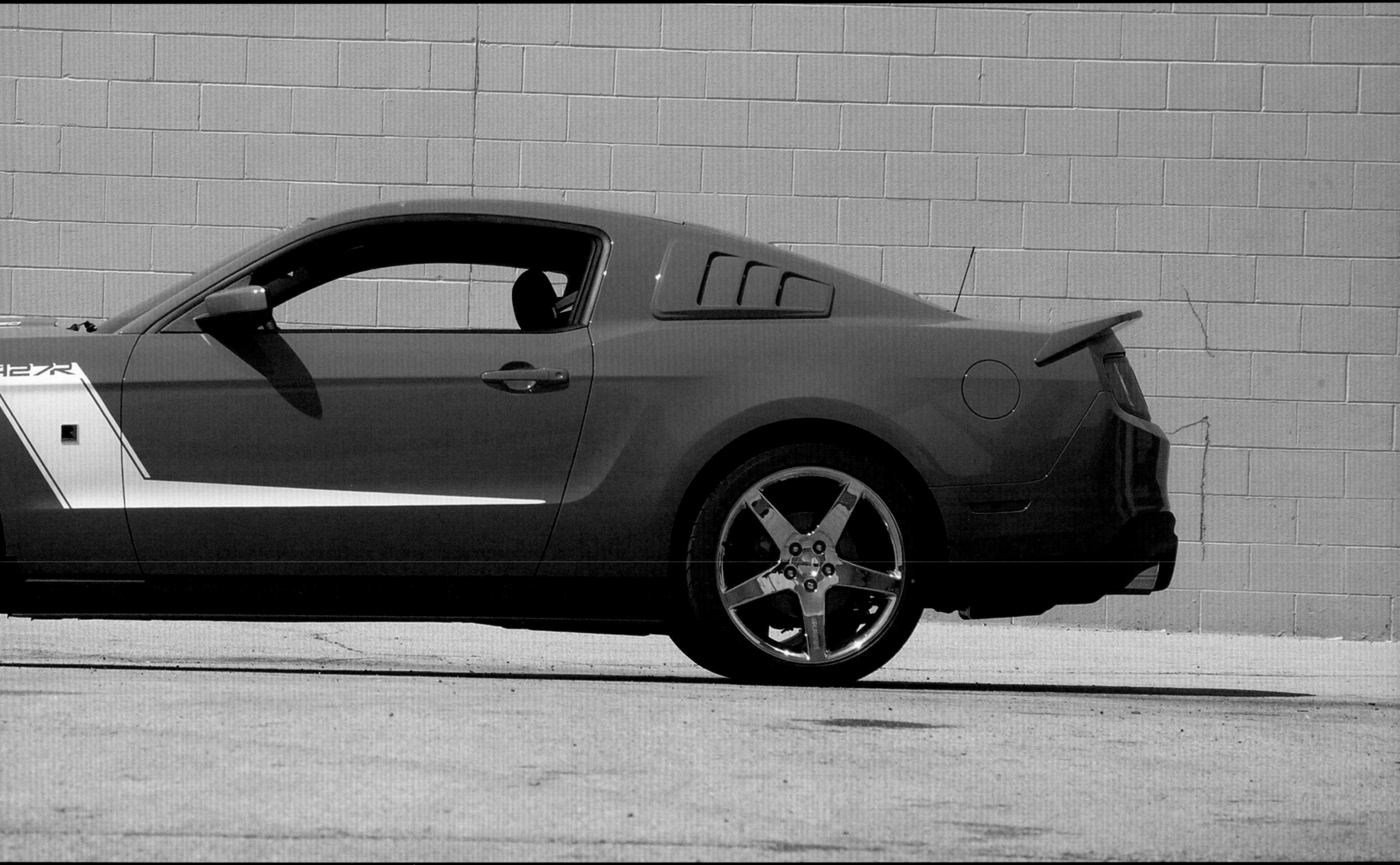
427R

But as interesting as the 427R might have been on a spec sheet, it was on the road that it shined best. According to *Motor Trend*, the 2010 427R would reach 60 mph from a stop in 4.7 seconds. Per *MT*, that was about two tenths of a second faster than a stock manual-transmission Mustang GT. While at first blush those numbers might have disappointed, it was important to note how much wheel spin needed to be overcome to have achieved anything like an efficient launch. All the torque this delightfully revvy engine produced was available immediately, utterly without the expected blower lag or hesitation.

Helping manage all this power was an optional short-throw shifter. This hefty, solid-feeling stickshift was a paragon of mechanical precision and smoothness that invited unneeded shifting simply because it was so much fun to manipulate.

This powertrain responsiveness became an allegory for the entire car. No Mustang, no matter how special or rare, had ever felt as much an extension of the driver as the 427R did.

The steering was direct and surprisingly light. The suspension upgrades resulted in a car that was not only light on its feet and absolutely flingable—in the best possible way—but one that actually rode more comfortably and with more composure than any stock Mustang.

All that said, the power, handling, and ride accounted for maybe half of what made the 427R so special. There was also the sound. The snorting, throbbing, menacing burble emitted from the 427R's exhaust was not only intoxicating, it was addictive, an aural tachometer that demanded unwarranted throttle blips no matter your actual power needs.

MUSTANG BOSS 302 2012

The original Ford Mustang Boss 302 was one of the best-loved Mustangs of all time, and for good reason. Offered only for 1969 and 1970, it was a homologation special produced so that Ford could face off against the rival Chevrolet Camaro Z/28 both in the showroom and on the track. Under the hood was a gutsy, high-winding 302-cid small-block V-8. The basic idea of a new-millennium revival of the Boss 302 was something of a no-brainer for Ford. The Mustang's 2005 redesign (and its 2010 reskin) brought a new-age-classic Mustang shape that pilfered cues from the celebrated 1967-70 Mustangs. Thus, that Mustang body was the perfect canvas for a revival of the original Boss 302's arresting paint colors and in-your-face stripes. The introduction of the fantastic "Coyote" 5.0-liter V-8 for the 2011 Mustang GT locked in the "302" part.

Ford decided that the new Boss 302 just couldn't be some halfhearted stickers-and-badges appearance package, and it wasn't. The Boss 302 got plenty of exclusive performance hardware above and beyond the already-potent base GT Mustang. The GT's 412-bhp V-8 was significantly massaged and upgraded to put out 444 horsepower at a high-winding 7,500 rpm. A new short-runner intake manifold, unique CNC-ported cylinder heads with larger and lighter exhaust valves, and more aggressive camshafts were just a few of the performance-enhancing revisions. A close-ratio six-speed manual (with a short-throw shifter) was the only available transmission. Substantial suspension revisions included high-rate springs, a slightly lower ride height, larger rear antiroll bar, lightweight 19-inch wheels with Pirelli PZero summer tires, and a heavy-duty version of the stock GT's available Brembo brake package.

Regular Boss 302s stickered for $40,995 with destination, but for a select group of weekend hot shoes who wanted a full-blown track-day machine from the factory, Ford offered a limited run of Boss 302 Laguna Seca editions. The $6995 Laguna Seca package included the Recaro seats and Torsen rear end that are optional on the base Boss, and added race-compound Pirelli Corsa tires on special lightweight 19-inch wheels, front-brake cooling ducts, a rear pedestal spoiler, a rigidity-enhancing cross-brace instead of a rear seat, and a dashtop gauge pod with engine-temperature, oil-pressure, and lateral-g gauges. An extra-aggressive front splitter was intended for track use, since it would almost certainly have been damaged on speed bumps, steep driveways, and the like.

Both Bosses delivered truly fabulous performance: Magazine road tests pegged 0–60 mph in the 4.0- to 4.3-second range, and quarter miles in 12.3 to 12.8 seconds. The naturally aspirated mill pulled smoothly and strongly all the way to its lofty redline. Furthermore, the Boss 302's overall balance and composure in aggressive driving were about as good as it got in a production live-rear-axle car. Laguna Seca versions topped 1g on the skidpad, with base Bosses not too far behind. *Car and Driver* summed up the Mustang Boss 302 with, "As automotive resurrections go, this is a knockout that venerates the original Boss while embarrassing it objectively and subjectively in every meaningful measure. What this is, is the best Mustang ever."

CHEVROLET
SS 2014–2016

When discussing the 2014-16 Chevrolet SS, it was impossible to ignore the one-year-and-out 2009 Pontiac G8 GXP. Killed off like all Pontiacs in the wake of General Motors's 2009 bankruptcy filing, the 415-bhp GXP was the highest-performance variant of Pontiac's new-for-2008 G8 based on GM's Holden Commodore VE from Australia.

Commodore production continued with versions of the car sold as Chevrolets in international markets. Around the time that Holden confirmed an updated Commodore VF model in 2013, GM issued word that a variant would come to America as the 2014 Chevrolet SS.

In the States, Chevrolet had been selling a long-wheelbase Commodore spin-off as the police-only Caprice PPV since 2011. However, like the departed G8, the new SS was based on the standard-length rear-wheel-drive Commodore. Thus it rested on a 114.8-inch wheelbase and was 195.5 inches long.

Americans were only offered well-equipped SS sedans priced from $44,470. The lone powerteam was a 415-horsepower 6.2-liter V-8 and six-speed automatic transmission. The suspension paired MacPherson struts up front with an independent multilink set-up out back. Brembo front brakes and forged 19-inch alloy wheels wearing sticky Bridgestone rubber were part of the deal too.

Exterior styling closely followed the updated Commodore. High-intensity-discharge headlamps and LED daytime running lights were standard. The hood and trunklid were aluminum to save a bit of weight. The nine-inch-wide rear wheels were .5-inch wider than the fronts, and wore bigger rubber. Five colors were available: Silver Ice Metallic, Red Hot 2, Phantom Black Metallic, Heron White, and Mystic Green Metallic.

All interiors had black leather upholstery and eight-way power front buckets. A Bose stereo was standard, along with Chevy's MyLink infotainment and touch-screen navigation. A power sunroof was one of the car's few options.

Road & Track tested an SS for its February 2014 issue, reporting a 0-60-mph time of 4.5 seconds and a quarter-mile dash of 12.9 seconds at better than 110 mph. *R&T* liked the balanced handling, and said the car "feels like an American version of the BMW M5." Gripes centered on the body's reserved styling and chrome accents.

The 2015 SS received GM's Magnetic Ride Control suspension and rear Brembo brakes as standard. Perhaps the biggest news was that a six-speed manual transmission packaged with a more aggressive 3.70:1 axle ratio joined the order sheet. New metallic colors were on an expanded palette, including Perfect Blue, Some Like it Hot Red, Alchemy Purple, Jungle Green, and Regal Peacock Green.

Chevy gave the 2016 SS a subtle styling update with a new front fascia and functional hood vents. The 19-inch wheels were cast rather than forged. There was also a new dual-mode exhaust system that allowed a throatier sound at full throttle. Slipstream Blue Metallic paint was in; Perfect Blue and Alchemy Purple were dropped.

GM announced that it would stop making cars in Australia by the end of 2017. In September 2015, Australian outlet *CarsGuide* reported that GM Asia-Pacific boss Stefan Jacoby confirmed the Chevrolet SS would be phased out and not directly replaced when production of the V-8-powered Commodore ended.

i8 2014–2019

Beginning with the 2009 introduction of its Vision Efficient Dynamics concept vehicle, BMW began teasing the idea of an exotic sports car with a high-tech, eco-conscious focus. After exploring the concept further (and introducing the i8 name) on a couple subsequent concept vehicles, the company officially committed to a production model—in September 2013, the i8 prototype was unveiled at the International Motor Show in Frankfurt, Germany.

The production i8 launched as a 2014 model, with unorthodox styling that covered an equally unconventional plug-in-hybrid powertrain. And almost all of the concept vehicles' outlandish features—most notably the scissor-wing doors—made the jump from the show floor to the showroom. The starting price was steep ($135,700 in the United States), but not unreasonable compared to similar luxury exotics.

The i8's gas-electric powertrain paired a turbocharged 1.5-liter 3-cylinder gasoline engine rated at 228 horsepower with a BMW-made synchronous electric motor that was good for 129 hp. Combined maximum output was 357 horsepower and 420 lb-ft of torque. The gasoline engine drove the rear wheels and was mated to a six-speed automatic transmission; the electric motor sent its power to the car's front wheels via a two-stage automatic transmission. Power for the electric motor was supplied by a liquid-cooled lithium-ion battery pack with a usable capacity of five kilowatt hours. The powertrain control software allowed the car to be operated on either power source independently or use both of them together, depending on the driving situation; the front-to-rear power split was also variable. BMW quoted the i8's 0–60-mph time at 4.2 seconds, and the EPA's gas-electric mileage estimate was 76 MPGe in combined city/highway driving.

Along with the smaller BMW i3 commuter vehicle, the i8 utilized BMW's LifeDrive architecture concept, which utilized independent "Life" and "Drive" structural modules. In the case of the i8, the Drive module was an aluminum structure that housed the gas and electric motors, the lithium-ion battery pack, chassis and suspension hardware, and the car's crash structure. The Life module consisted of the car's CFRP (carbon-fiber reinforced plastic) passenger cabin. The i8 was 184.6 inches long, 76.5 inches wide, and 51 inches tall, with a curb weight of 3285 pounds.

The interior used a sports-car-typical low seating position. The cabin's appearance followed the layered approach used on the body, along with the imaginative use of contrasting colors. A mix of leathers, cloth accents, painted surfaces, and exposed carbon fiber added to the ambiance. The driver could choose from five driving modes using the Driving Experience Control switch and eDrive button.

Consumer Guide® Automotive editors tested a 2015 i8, and were impressed by the car's balance of ride comfort and sporty handling, as well as its vivacious acceleration and throttle response. However, the swoopy, low-slung styling and radical doors didn't do any favors for ease of entry and exit or visibility.

BMW announced several updates for the 2019 i8, including the addition of a two-seat roadster variant to be sold alongside the coupe. Other upgrades included an increase of total gas/electric output to 369 horsepower, and an updated lithium-ion battery pack that increased capacity (BMW said net capacity was 9.4 kilowatt hours) and range. There were also some new interior trim choices and exterior colors. Coupe prices started at $147,500, and the new Roadster model had a base price of $163,300.

ALFA ROMEO
4C 2015–2016

Alfa Romeo's long-promised return to the American market had seemingly been in the works since imports of the 164 sedan had ended in 1995. Maserati dealers sold Americans about 100 $250,000-plus Alfa 8Cs between 2008 and 2010. But more attainable models were only promised, not delivered. Finally, after countless delays, the first examples of the Alfa Romeo 4C hit the company's small network of Stateside dealers in late 2014.

Not exactly mainstream, the 4C was a small, two-seat, mid-engine sports car that was built at corporate cousin Maserati's plant in Modena, Italy. The main section of the chassis is a tub made of carbon-fiber that remained visible in the car's interior. Roof reinforcements and a frame that mounts the engine were aluminum, as were the fr.................. The bodywork was formed from .... .C rode on a 93.7-inch

The 4C'..
was an ..
and 258
transmis
"DNA" ....
altered e...

The horsepower number was modest by today's standards, but the coupe's claimed 2,465-pound curb weight helped. *Road & Track* reported a 0–60-mph time of 4.2 seconds and a quarter-mile run of 12.8 seconds at 108.2 mph.

The first of the American-market 4Cs were Launch Edition coupes in a run of just 500 cars. These had additional interior and exterior carbon-fiber accent pieces, black microfiber and leather interior trim with red or white contrast-stitch detailing, side air intakes on the front fascia, and a serial-numbered plaque. Performance enhancements included "race" exhaust and suspension tuning, along with 18-inch front and 19-inch rear wheels and tires. Base price was $68,400.

A "base" 4C coupe came later with smaller 17- and 18-inch rubber, less equipment, and a $53,900 starting price. The 2015 lineup also included a $63,900 4C Spider with a removable reinforced-fabric roof panel. The 2,487-pound Spider also introduced interior updates that included additional small-item storage spots and an Alpine-brand audio system. These appreciated tweaks helped mitigate complaints about the early cars, especially the roundly panned Parrot-brand stereo.

For 2016, the 4C coupe received the Spider's interior updates and Alpine head unit. There were new interior trim choices for both cars too.

For the hard-core sports-car lover, this exotic Italian was relatively affordable. The car's surprising mixture of high-tech materials and back-to-basics personality offered an undeniably compelling character as well.

CHALLENGER SRT HELLCAT 2015

The SRT Hellcat was a complete monster that was arguably defined by one thing—a 707-bhp supercharged 6.2-liter Hemi V-8. At the time, the mightiest Chevrolet Camaro, the supercharged ZL1, was rated at "only" 580 ponies. The 2014 Shelby GT500 Mustang was rated at 662. Even Dodge's 640-horsepower SRT Viper sports car was upstaged.

Dodge said Hellcat was the most powerful muscle car ever. It was one of the most powerful cars sold in the U.S. If you needed more power, you had to shop a very select group including the Ferrari F12 (730 bhp) and the gas-electric-hybrid Porsche 918 Spyder (887 bhp).

Hellcats didn't look all that different than other SRT Challengers. There was a unique grille that did not share the other models' new split-grille theme inspired by the 1971 Challenger. Hellcats also boasted an aluminum hood with a pair of air-extractor vents flanking the central scoop, a specific front fascia with splitter, larger rear spoiler, and "Supercharged" badges on the front fenders. Interior tweaks included red gauge lighting and engine-turned aluminum trim.

The supercharged Hemi was related to Dodge's unblown 6.4-liter mill, but Dodge said the engines actually shared fewer than 10 percent of their parts. Hellcat upgrades included a specific cast-iron block, forged-steel crankshaft, forged-alloy pistons, forged powdered-metal connecting rods, and specific alloy heads.

The twin-screw supercharger gulped air from a port integrated into the driver's side inboard "headlamp." Other enhancements were an upgraded fuel pump, .5-inch diameter fuel lines, high-capacity engine-oil cooler, and two intercoolers that helped control intake-air temperatures.

A six-speed manual transmission with an external oil cooler and a heavy-duty clutch was standard. A heavy-duty eight-speed TorqueFlite automatic was optional. It came with steering-wheel-mounted shift paddles.

Chassis upgrades extended to the driveshaft, rear axle, and half shafts. Bearings and rear-axle gears were also upgraded to handle the Hellcat's fury. Up front there were new 15.4-inch Brembo-brand brake rotors with six-piston calipers. Hellcats rode on 9.5-inch-wide 20-inch wheels wrapped in speed-rated Pirelli tires.

Driver-selected "Drive Modes"—Default, Sport, and Track—controlled engine power, traction control, automatic-transmission shift speed, and suspension stiffness. Enthusiasts could mix characteristics from the modes via a Custom setting. There was also a Launch Control feature to help get all 707 ponies to the ground as efficiently as possible.

Hellcats came with two keys. The red one accessed the car's full performance potential. A black key limited engine output to around 500 bhp. A Valet setting further restricted performance.

Muscle cars—especially ones with 707 bhp—and the drag strip were made for each other. Hellcat could lay down a National Hot Rod Association-certified quarter-mile run of 11.2 seconds on the stock street tires or 10.8 seconds with drag radials. *Motor Trend* reported a 0-60-mph time of 3.7 seconds with the automatic and a second-gear start.

BMW
M2 2016–2017

In 2014 BMW replaced the 1-Series as its premium subcompact in America. The new holder of that job was the 2-Series. The basic idea here was a coupe or convertible with four seats and rear drive. There were two subseries, the 228i with a turbocharged four and the M235i with a 320-bhp turbocharged inline six.

What was missing at the time was a full performance version from BMW's M division. That gap was filled in 2016 when the Bavarians brought out the M2 coupe.

To make it, the M235i's 3.0-liter six was reworked and received the pistons and crankshaft main-bearing shells from the engine used in the larger M3 and M4. The oil supply was tweaked to ensure proper lubrication under heavy acceleration and braking, and the cooling system was upgraded. Fitted with a single twin-scroll turbocharger, the M2's heart was rated at 365 bhp.

The standard transmission was a six-speed manual. It came with an automatic rev-matching feature that electronically blipped the throttle for downshifts. (Some buff-book reviewers bemoaned that rev matching could only be disabled by turning off the car's stability-control system.) A seven-speed dual-clutch transmission—"M DCT with Drivelogic" in BMW-speak—was optional. This gearbox allowed for automatic operation, or the driver could shift gears manually without using a clutch pedal. BMW quoted a 0-60-mph time of 4.2 seconds with the DCT, and 4.4 with the traditional stick.

M2's disc brakes and aluminum-intensive front and rear suspensions were borrowed from the M3 and M4. The 19-inch forged wheels were nine inches wide in front, 10 inches wide in the rear, and wore Michelin Pilot Super Sport rubber.

The M2 bowed at 176.2-inches long, rode a 106-inch wheelbase, and had a curb weight of 3,450 pounds with manual transmission. For comparison, a 2017 Chevrolet Camaro was 188.3 inches from nose to tail on a 110.7-inch wheelbase, and weighed 3,463 pounds with a V-6 and manual trans.

M2 bodywork deviated substantially from the standard 2-Series cars. Front and rear fenders were dramatically bulged to accommodate the car's wider tracks and sticky Michelins. The car also wore model-specific front and rear fascias, along with a modest lip spoiler on the trunklid.

BMW cataloged few options for the M2. Alpine White was the only "free" paint choice. Alternatives were the extra-cost metallic Long Beach Blue, Black Sapphire, or Mineral Grey. Interiors were trimmed in black leather with contrasting blue stitching. Accents included "open-pore carbon fiber" trim and some Alcantara-covered bits. There was also an Executive Package that added a heated steering wheel, rearview camera, and some driver-assistance items.

The introductory starting price of $51,700 jumped to $52,695 for 2017. Changes for '17 were the additions of wireless smartphone charging and a Wi-Fi hotspot to the Executive Package. There was a new $2,500 M Driver's Package that increased top speed to 168 mph (from 155) and included a driver-training course at a BMW Performance Center in South Carolina or California.

There are supercars, and then there are supercars, and the Bugatti Chiron definitely qualifies as the latter. The Chiron's quad-turbocharged 8.0-liter W-16 engine developed an astonishing 1500 horsepower and 1180 pound-feet of torque—enough for a 0-60 mph time of 2.4 seconds and an electronically limited top speed of 261 mph. A Haldex all-wheel-drive system got all that power to the road with the least amount of drama. The Chiron set a world record by accelerating 0 to 400 km/h (248 mph) and then braking to a stop in 41.96 seconds. That record was quickly bettered by Koenigsegg, but it was still a remarkable accomplishment. Base price for the Chiron was around $3,000,000. As expected at that price, there was no visible plastic in the cockpit—only top-grade leather and metal. The Chiron was more refined and quiet than its predecessor, the Bugatti Veyron, and was also surprisingly docile at low speeds.

CAMARO ZL1 2017–2018

Chevrolet celebrated the Camaro's 50th anniversary in 2017. There was a commemorative model with special trim, but more importantly there was a high-performance ZL1.

The original Camaro ZL1 dates to 1969. Available by special order through Chevy's Central Office Production Order system, the first ZL1 was a dragstrip terror powered by a shockingly expensive all-aluminum 427-cid "big-block" V-8. Only sixty-nine were produced. Modern-day ZL1 history began in 2012, when the name was revived for an all-around performance Camaro powered by a supercharged 580-bhp 6.2-liter V-8.

Camaro was redesigned for 2016. The sixth-generation model closely followed the appearance of the well-received fifth-gen car, and was based on the General Motors "Alpha" rear-drive platform shared with Cadillac's ATS and CTS. Perhaps most significantly, the new Camaro was lighter and marginally smaller than the car it replaced.

The latest ZL1 debuted for 2017 in coupe and convertible forms. Unique exterior styling touches included wider front fenders, a vented hood, larger front splitter, and a rear wing. Power came from the LT4 supercharged 6.2-liter V-8 good for 650 horsepower and 650 pound-feet of torque. It could be backed by a six-speed manual transmission with an active rev-matching function or a Hydra-Matic ten-speed automatic. Other upgrades included a specifically tuned "Magnetic Ride" adaptable suspension, Brembo-brand brakes, 20-inch forged aluminum wheels, and ZL1-specific Goodyear Eagle F1 Supercar rubber. Weight was down 200 pounds compared to the previous ZL1.

Chevy-supplied performance numbers were a 0–60-mph time of 3.5 seconds, a quarter-mile sprint of 11.4 seconds at 127 mph, and a cornering limit of 1.02g. *Motor Trend* duplicated Chevy's 0–60 mark, but the best it could do in the quarter was 11.5 seconds at 125 mph. Still, that's .2 quicker than *MT* coaxed out of a Dodge Challenger Hellcat. *Car and Driver* said "it's a car you can live with every day and hustle across any piece of pavement, and we wouldn't change a thing."

For 2018, the ZL1 added a new coupe-only 1LE variant focused on racetrack performance. It added specific aerodynamic features to increase downforce, including air deflectors and dive planes up front and a carbon-fiber rear wing. The suspension was upgraded with what Chevrolet called "Multimatic DSSV" (Dynamic Suspension Spool Valve) dampers, adjustable front ride height and camber, and a three-way-adjustable rear stabilizer bar. The 1LE also wore wider, and lighter, 19-inch forged wheels and specially designed Goodyear Eagle F1 Supercar 3R tires. Chevy said the 3,820-pound curb weight is about sixty pounds lighter than a base ZL1 coupe thanks to the suspension and wheel changes, thinner rear glass, and a fixed rear seat back.

Visual cues marking the 1LE included a satin-black hood, black side mirrors and wheels, and darkened taillamps. The LT4 engine was unchanged, but 1LE only came with a six-speed manual gearbox running a model-specific top-gear ratio. Chevy asserted the ZL1 1LE was three seconds a lap faster than a standard ZL1 coupe when tested at GM's Milford Road Course test track.

The 2017 ZL1 coupe was priced from $62,135, with the convertible starting at $69,135. The 2018s were up to $63,795 and $69,795, respectively. The 1LE package added $7,500 to the coupe's bottom line.

For Camaro's 50th anniversary, Chevy's best present to Camaro fans was the ZL1. It was crazy fast in a straight line or on a road course, while still impressing the buff-books on the street.

DODGE
VIPER 2017

When the production version of the original Dodge Viper RT/10 was introduced for the 1992 model year, it really was like nothing else. Sure Carroll Shelby's legendary Sixties-era Ford-powered Cobras provided inspiration but Viper's in-your-face all-American design and 400-bhp V-10 engine captured the public's imagination.

Twenty-five years later, Viper's basic layout remained unchanged but the V-10 was rated at 645 bhp, which made the '92 model seem downright tame by comparison. Regardless, Viper had been a slow seller in its last years and Dodge announced that production would end with the 2017 models.

The previous Viper's run ended in 2010, but Chrysler's bankruptcy pushed off its replacement to the 2013 model year. The '13 was a bit better equipped than previous snakes, but otherwise was very familiar to Viper fans. That meant that it wasn't daily-driver friendly, but the payoff was a brutally powerful track-focused sports car.

Arguably the most significant news was that the car was being sold under Chrysler's SRT performance-vehicle brand so it was technically no longer a Dodge. Another development was the discontinuation of the open-top model; all Vipers were coupes.

Disappointing sales led to a rethink, and 2015 Vipers were once again titled as Dodges. There was also a substantial price cut including a $15,000 reduction for the base model. These changes didn't improve the model's fortunes, and annual sales totals remained stuck in the hundreds.

The 2017 Viper lineup was crazy complicated and included SRT, GTC, GTS, and ACR (American Club Racer) models. Prices started at $87,895 for the SRT and went up to $118,795 for the ACR. Then there were six special limited-edition models: Snakeskin Edition GTC (25 units, $118,890 base price), 1:28 Edition ACR (28 units, $143,890), Snakeskin Edition ACR (31 units), Voodoo II Edition ACR (31 units, $141,190), GTS-R Commemorative Edition ACR (100 units, $145,340), and Dodge Dealer Edition ACR (22 units). This last special was only offered through Tomball Dodge in Texas and Roanoke Dodge in Illinois.

Dodge also offered a "1 of 1" personalized customization program for Viper GTC and ACR models. There was an almost-endless choice of 16,000 paint colors and 48,000 stripe combinations, not to mention other tweaks that included seven different aero packages, four suspension setups, and eleven different wheel styles. Dodge said all this added up to more than 50 million possible configurations, and that choosing to take part in the 1 of 1 program guaranteed "a truly one-of-a-kind hand built American supercar" that included a personalized dashboard badge.

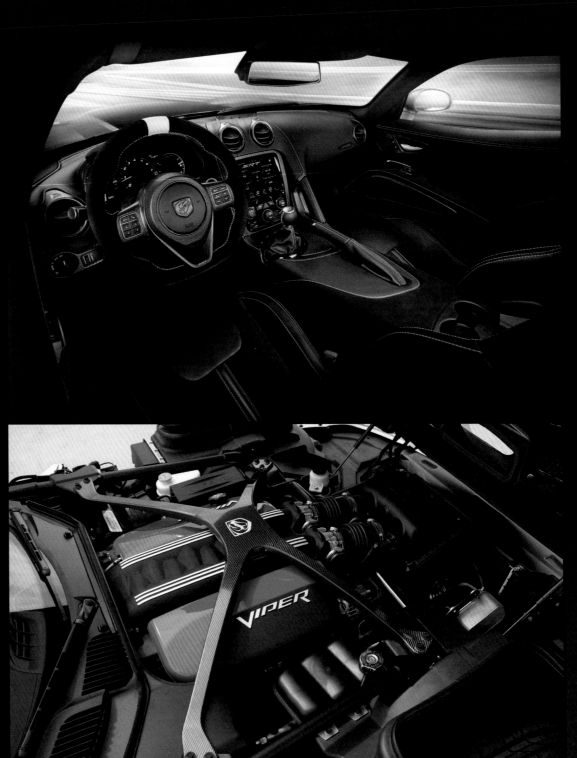

FERRARI

LAFERRARI 2017

Ferrari would probably be the last make expected to sell a hybrid, but the LaFerrari was no ordinary hybrid—it combined a 788-horsepower V-12 with a 161-hp electric motor for a total 949 hp. Introduced for 2013, the LaFerrari hybrid was even faster than Ferrari's celebrated 2003-04 Enzo model— could rocket from 0-60 mph in less than three seconds and hit a top speed of 217 mph. Plus, the weight of the low-mounted battery packs lowered the car's center of gravity and improved handling. The LaFerrari's price tag was a cool $1.4 million, but Ferrari had no trouble selling 500 coupes, as well as 210 Aperta convertible versions. The final LaFerrari Aperta was sold at an auction in 2017 for $9.96 million, with proceeds supporting the Save the Children charity.

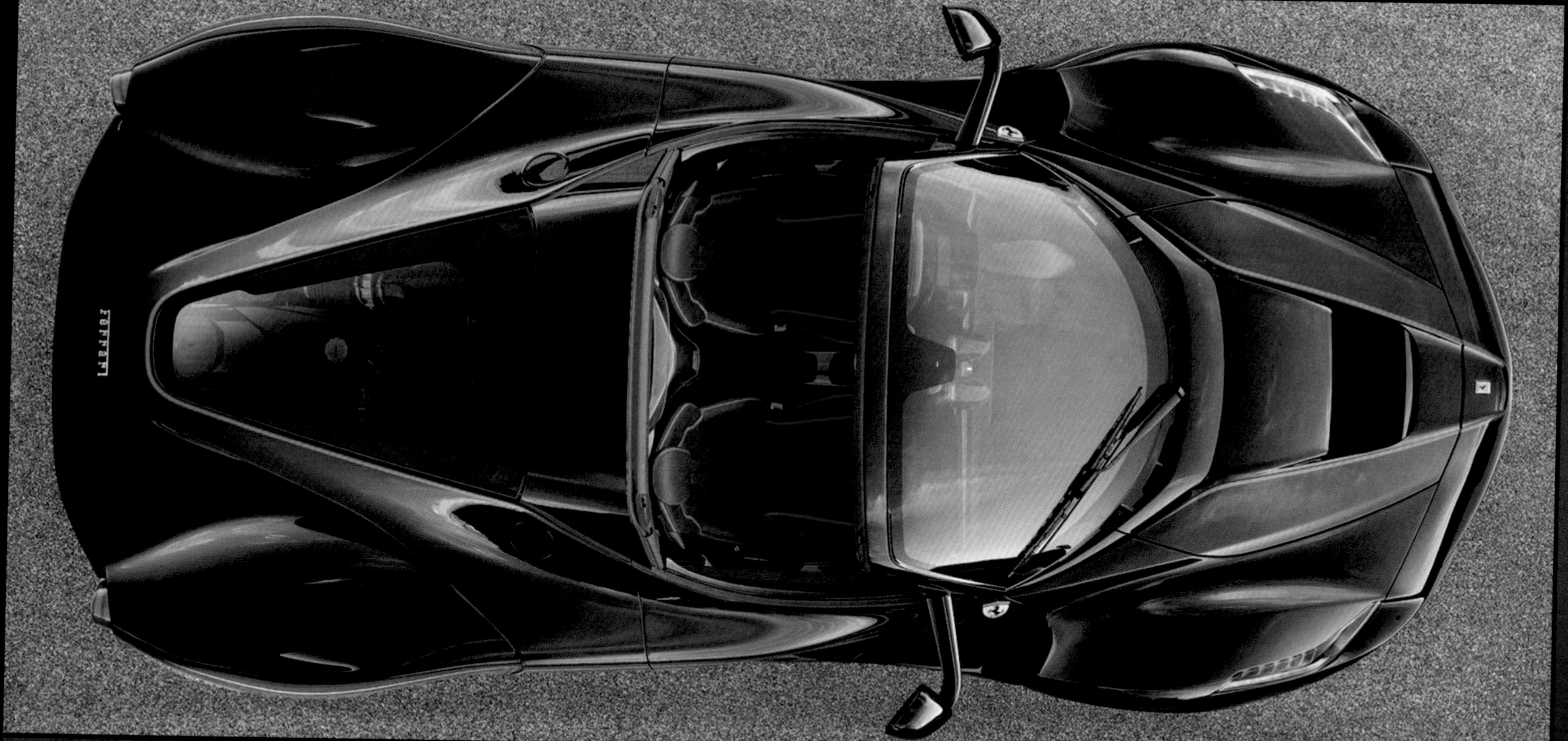

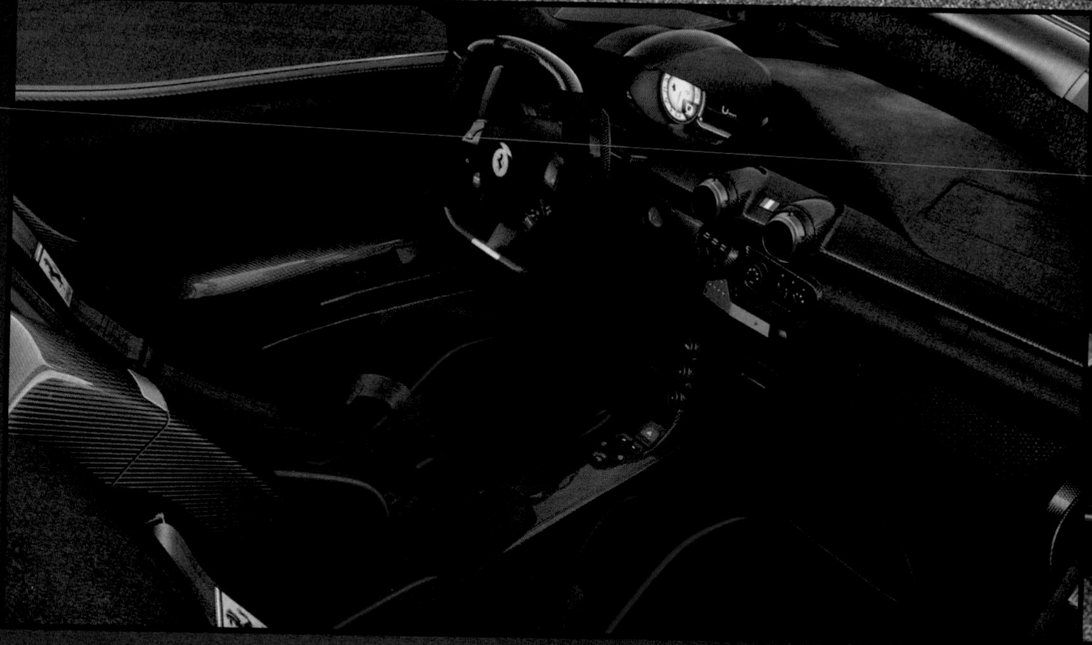

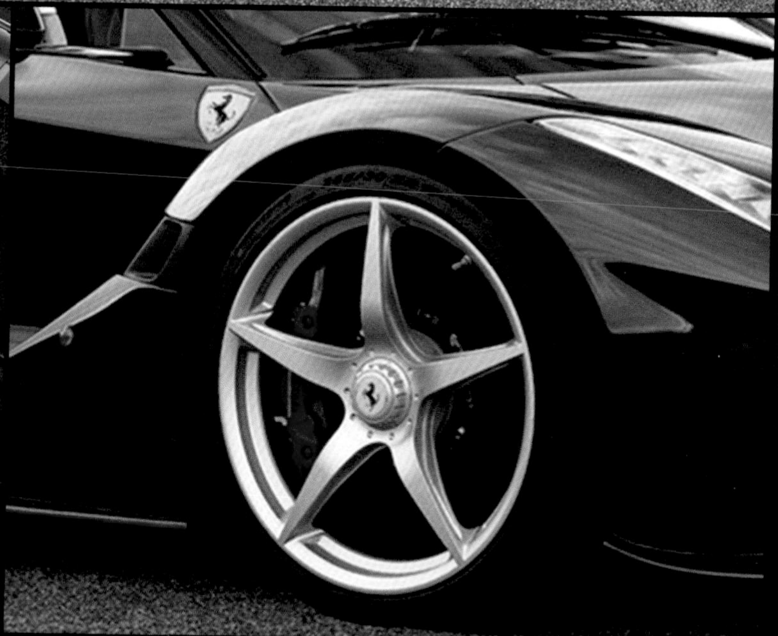

GT 2017

To celebrate the 50th anniversary of the Ford GT40's historic 1966 Le Mans victory, Ford designed an all-new GT racecar for the 2016 24 Hours of Le Mans. The new GTs did their legendary forebears proud, finishing first, third, fourth, and ninth in the GTE Pro Class. The production GT was closely related to the racing version, and lacked the luxury features often found on other high-end supercars. The GT's cockpit was a tight fit for two passengers, and cargo room was almost nonexistent. The payoff was reduced weight, with racecar-like performance and handling. The EcoBoost 3.5-liter V6 shared its basic engine block with the Ford F-150, but developed 647 horsepower and was capable of traveling from 0-60 mph in 2.9 seconds and reaching a top speed of 216 mph, according to *Car and Driver*. The price was around $450,000, and Ford planned to build 1000 examples over the 2017–2020 model years.

AGERA RS 2017-2018

The story of Swedish supercar maker Koenigsegg traces back to 1994 when the company was founded by the then 22-year-old Christian von Koenigsegg. According to a company-supplied history, the founder's dream was to create the perfect supercar. The original Koenigsegg CC prototype was created by the company's small team of craftsmen and shown at the Cannes Film Festival in 1997. Series production of the CC8S followed in 2002.

Following a fire at the company's original building, the firm moved into its present facility in 2003. Located in Ängelholm, Sweden, the building was originally used by the Swedish Air Force and served as home base for one of the country's jet-fighter squadrons. The adjacent runway provided ample space for high-speed testing.

Koenigsegg's Agera model debuted in 2010. The company says "*Agera* means 'to take action' in Swedish." Of interest here is the Agera RS, which was originally shown at Geneva in March 2015. They claimed it to be "designed as a road-legal car with a track focus." The company announced that twenty-five cars would be built, with ten of them pre-sold prior to the first showing. Prices likely started well north of a million U.S. dollars.

The Agera's tub was hand assembled in Koenigsegg's workshop from carbon fiber and an aluminum honeycomb core. Bodywork is carbon fiber as well. The car is approximately 169 inches long, runs a 104.8-inch wheelbase, and is 44.1 inches tall. Curb weight is 3,075 pounds.

Another of the Agera's defining features was the firm's Dihedral Sychrohelix door hinge. The company described this hinge as opening the "door outwards and upwards in one smooth, sweeping motion." They also claimed this system delivered the practical benefits of needing less horizontal space to open the door than a traditional setup, and less vertical space than a gullwing or scissor door.

The engine was a Koenigsegg-developed 32-valve twin-turbocharged 5.0-liter V-8. It was rated at 1,160 horsepower and 944 lb-ft of torque. An optional "1MW" version of the engine raised the stakes to 1,360 horsepower and 1011 lb-ft of twist. The transmission was a seven-speed sequential unit.

The suspension used double wishbones at both ends, along with electronically adjustable Ohlins dampers. The rear suspension also integrated a "Triplex" third damper that Koenigsegg said provided resistance to rear-end "squat" under heavy acceleration. Wheels were Koenigsegg's Aircore units that were hollow carbon fiber pieces.

Factory supplied performance numbers with the 1MW engine were 0–62 mph in 2.8 seconds and 0–186 mph in 12.3 seconds. On October 1, 2017, a U.S.-spec Agera RS with the 1MW engine driven by a factory driver, accelerated from 0 to 400 kilometers an hour (approximately 248.5 mph) and then decelerated back to 0 in 36.44 seconds. The test took place at an airfield in Denmark.

On November 4, the same car set several speed records on a closed section of Highway 160 outside of Pahrump, Nevada. Highlights included a one-way run of 284.55 mph, and an average speed of 276.36 mph over a mile run in both directions.

ASTON MARTIN
VALKYRIE 2018

Aston Martin partnered with Red Bull Racing of Formula 1 fame to develop an all-new hypercar called the Valkyrie. When first revealed in July 2016, the car was referred to by its codename, AM-RB 001 ("AM" for Aston Martin, and "RB for Red Bull). In March 2017, the Valkyrie name—inspired by the Norse mythological figure—was announced.

The Valkyrie was designed by Red Bull Racing's Chief Technical Officer, Adrian Newey. The form-follows-function exterior styling is a result of Newey's focus on downforce and aerodynamic efficiency; Aston Martin claimed the car "boasts truly radical aerodynamics for unprecedented levels of downforce in a road-legal car," and said that much of the car's aerodynamic downforce was generated by the design of the underside Venturi tunnels.

Noteworthy styling details included exposed headlight assemblies and mounting brackets, a chemically etched aluminum Aston Martin badge on the car's nose that was thinner than a human hair and buried under a coat of clear lacquer, and what was claimed to be the world's smallest center-mount brake light.

The interior filled the space between the car's underbody aero tunnels. Modern-day racecar design provided inspiration, and the cockpit's ergonomics were decidedly minimalist. The seats were mounted directly to the chassis tub, with driver and passenger seated in a reclined position with their legs outstretched in front of them. All switchgear was located on the removable steering wheel, and the car's virtual instrumentation was presented on a lone display screen. Traditional rear-view mirrors were replaced with rear-facing cameras and small monitor screens mounted at each end of the dash.

At the Geneva Motor Show in March 2018, Aston Martin and Red Bull introduced the track-only Valkyrie AMR Pro. Weighing in at 1,000 kilograms (about 2,200 pounds), the car featured numerous weight-saving measures, including lighter-weight carbon-fiber bodywork, polycarbonate windows, carbon-fiber suspension wishbones, race seats, and a lighter exhaust system. In addition, interior comfort and convenience pieces were deleted.

The 6.5-liter naturally aspirated V-12 engine and its hybrid-electric "Energy Recovery System" were tweaked to provide 1,100 horsepower. Top track speed was a claimed 225 mph, and the car was said to be capable of lateral acceleration in excess of 3Gs. Deliveries were expected to begin in 2020, but the company said that the twenty-five examples they planned to build were already sold.

720S 2018

Bruce McLaren (1937–1970) was a racing driver from Auckland, New Zealand. He raced for the Cooper Car Company beginning in 1958, and while still with the team started his own outfit, Bruce McLaren Motor Racing, in 1963. The first McLaren racing machine was the M1A sports car of 1964. Formula 1 open wheelers soon followed, along with a series of ever-evolving Can-Am race cars powered by monstrous big-block Chevrolet engines.

Following Bruce McLaren's death in a Can-Am testing accident, the team continued to race, and went on to achieve victories in the Indianapolis 500 and Formula 1 in the 1970s. Ron Dennis entered the picture in 1980 as the head of an investment group that bought out the company, and led the team to even greater success. The first F1 car with a carbon-fiber composite tub, the McLaren MP4/1, debuted in 1981, and the company entered the road-car market with the 1993 McLaren F1. Surrey, England-based McLaren Automotive launched in 2010, and its first road car was the 2011 McLaren 12C.

At the Geneva Motor Show in March 2017, McLaren Automotive introduced its second-generation Super Series car, the 2018 McLaren 720S. It replaced the 650S, and was lighter and faster than its predecessor. Like all other McLaren road cars starting with the F1, the 720S was built on a carbon-fiber tub; this iteration was called the McLaren Monocage II. Bodywork was a combination of carbon fiber and aluminum. The 720S rode a 105-inch wheelbase, was 179 inches long, and had a curb weight of 3,128 pounds.

Exterior styling was an evolution of the McLaren look. Highlights included slim roof pillars that enhanced occupant visibility and taut "shrink-wrapped" bodywork. The dihedral doors were double skinned, which allowed them to hide inner ducting that channeled air to the car's radiators and eliminated the need for open side intakes.

The company touted the interior's "perception of space," promising comfortable seating for two along with enough room for an airline carry-on bag behind each seat. Leather trim by Bridge of Weir, machined aluminum switches, and an available Bowers & Wilkins audio system were other high-end accoutrements. The eight-inch Central Infotainment Screen allowed for many of the car's functions to be controlled by touch.

The mid-engine, rear-drive 720S ran McLaren's M480T twin-turbocharged 4.0-liter V-8, which was rated at 710 horsepower and 568 lb-ft of torque. The engine was mated to a seven-speed dual-clutch SSG (seamless-shift gearbox) transmission.

The sophisticated suspension used a double-wishbone setup in both the front and rear, as well as a new generation of McLaren's Proactive Chassis Control (with driver-selectable Comfort, Sport, or Track settings). The brakes paired carbon-ceramic discs with six-piston calipers.

McLaren estimated the 720S was capable of a 0–60-mph time of 2.8 seconds and a quarter-mile sprint of 10.3 seconds. Top speed was a claimed 212 mph. *Car and Driver* was impressed with the car's performance and day-to-day livability, but griped that the touchscreen infotainment system was not up to the standard of "ordinary" cars.

McLaren offered the 720S in three versions—in addition to the standard model, there were Performance and Luxury variants. McLaren also cataloged individual options along with so-called "option packs," and buyers could choose from twenty standard colors. American-market prices started at a cool $288,845.

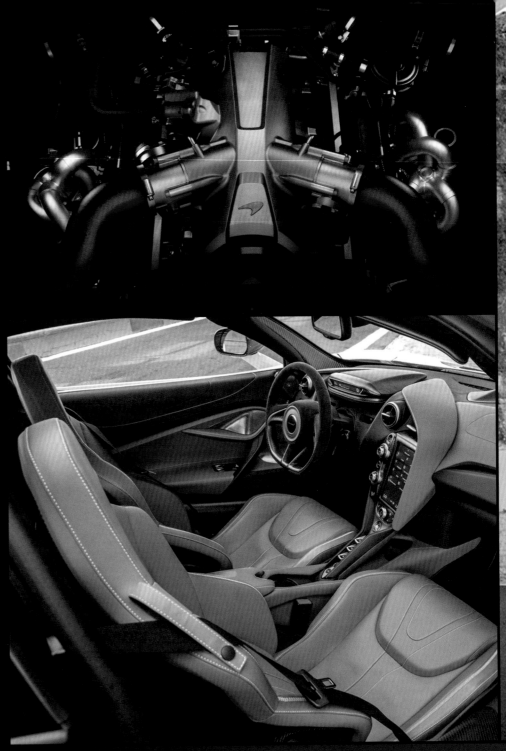

CHEVROLET
CORVETTE ZR1 2019

Chevrolet's Corvette sports car has a long, storied history filled with breathtaking acceleration and handling, groundbreaking styling innovations, and even legendary option codes. One of those codes—ZR1—has come to mean ultimate performance, Corvette style.

The first Corvette ZR1 appeared in 1970, and it was essentially a race-ready option package. Highlights of the package included the solid-lifter LT1 350-cubic-inch small-block V-8, heavy-duty four-speed transmission, and a tweaked suspension. Since the ZR1 was meant for the track, comfort items like power windows, air conditioning, and a radio weren't available. Chevy produced the ZR1 in very limited numbers from 1970–72.

The ZR-1 name reappeared (this time with a hyphen) for 1990, as the so-called "King of the Hill" Corvette. Technically a $27,016 option for the Corvette coupe, the main attraction was an all-aluminum LT5 dohc 5.7-liter V-8 good for a substantial 375 horsepower (for comparison, the base L98 5.7 made 245 ponies in 1990). The rear bodywork and rear wheels and tires were wider, and there was a new six-speed-manual transmission. Styling was touched up for 1991, and for 1993 the LT5's output was bumped up to 405 hp. Production of this generation of the ZR-1 ended after 1995.

The ZR1 was back for 2009, however, based on the aluminum frame developed for the 2006 Corvette Z06. The big news this time around was a supercharged LS9 6.2-liter V-8 rated at an eye-opening 638 horsepower. A six-speed manual was the only transmission available, and, like the Z06, the ZR1 was offered only as a coupe with a fixed roof panel. The initial base price was $103,300, and production continued through 2013.

In November 2017, Chevrolet introduced the 2019 ZR1 coupe at the Dubai Motor Show, and quickly followed it up with a convertible variant unveiled at the Los Angeles Auto Show. Easily eclipsing the '09 ZR1, the new model boasted a supercharged 755-horsepower LT5 6.2-liter V-8. Engineering highlights included a larger-displacement blower than the one on the Z06, and a dual-fuel-injection system that supplemented the primary direct-injection setup with port injectors. Buyers could choose a seven-speed manual or eight-speed automatic transmission; the available automatic was a first for ZR1. Chevy claimed a ZR1 equipped with the automatic was capable of 0–60-mph times of less than three seconds and quarter-mile runs in the high-ten-second range.

Other ZR1 features included an upgraded cooling system that worked with a new front fascia, a specific carbon-fiber hood, and two specially developed aerodynamic packages. The standard aero setup used a so-called "Low Wing" in back and allowed for the car's highest top speed, claimed to be 212 miles per hour. The optional $2,995 ZTK Performance Package added an adjustable "High Wing," front splitter, Michelin Pilot Sport Cup 2 summer performance tires, and specific tuning for the chassis and Magnetic Ride Control. Both rear wings sat on stanchions that were mounted to the car's chassis, similar to the setup on the Corvette C7.R racecar.

There was also a new Sebring Orange Design Package that started with a dazzling Sebring Orange tintcoat paint finish. Orange highlights extended to the brake calipers, accent striping, seat belts, and interior stitch detailing. The 2019 Corvette ZR1 coupe's base price was $119,995, while the convertible started at $123,995.

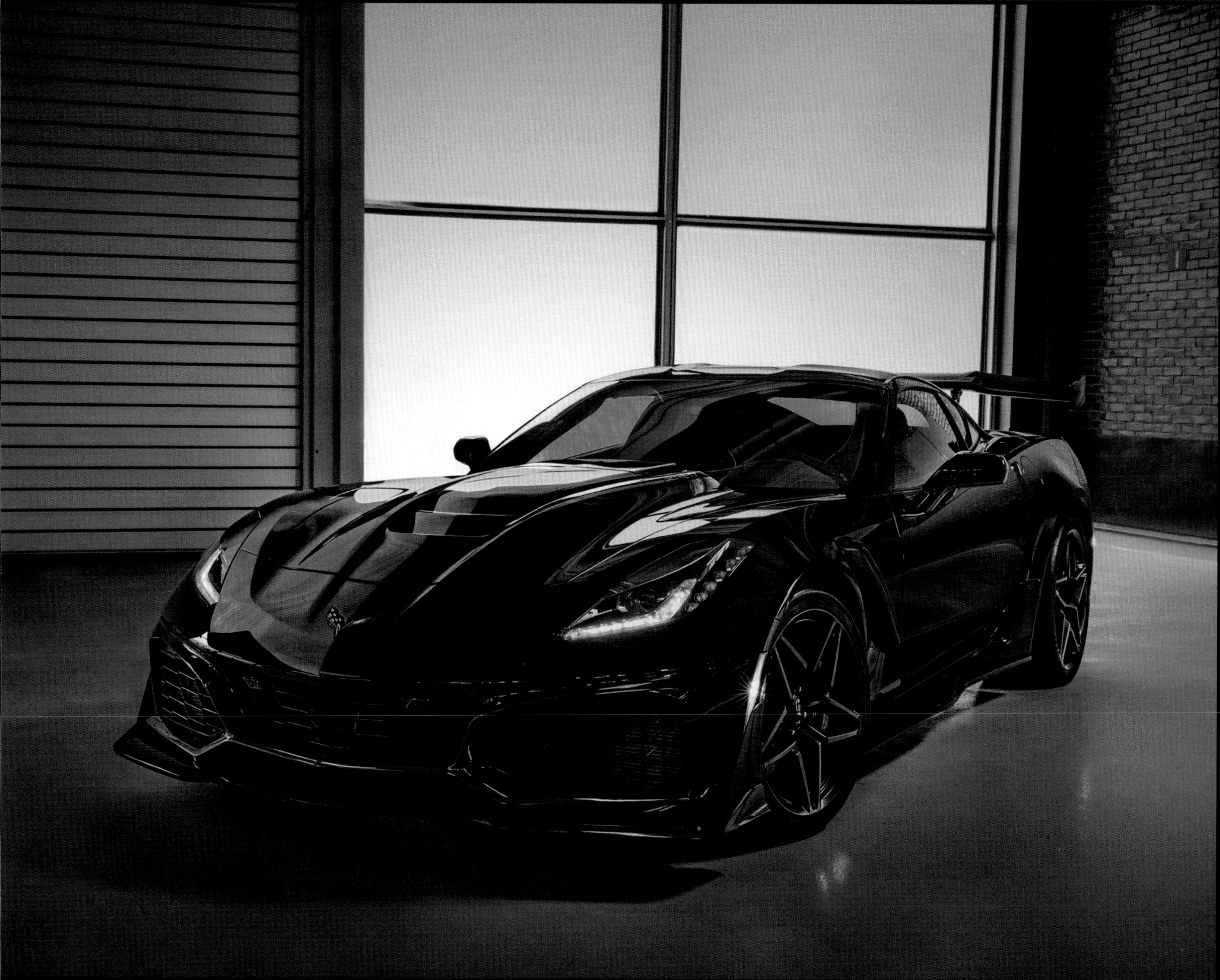

MCLAREN
SENNA 2019

The McLaren Senna was a testament to the company's racing heritage. Founder Bruce McLaren was a New Zealand born driver who started building English racecars in 1963. Legendary Brazilian driver Ayrton Senna raced for McLaren from 1988 to 1993, racking up three Formula One world championships. He was tragically killed while driving for another team in 1994.

The McLaren Senna was built as an uncompromising track car that could set fast lap times, yet was street legal. The Senna was based on the 720S. While the 720S was comfortable and docile for a mid-engine supercar, the track-focused Senna had firmer suspension and lacked sound insulation. All unnecessary weight was eliminated. The 2641-pound car was powered by a 789-horsepower twin-turbocharged 4.0-liter V8 and was capable of a top speed of 208 mph. Acceleration times were: 0-62 mph (100km/h) in 2.8 seconds, 0-124 mph (200km/h) in 6.8 seconds, and 0-186 mph (300km/h) in 17.5 seconds. Strong brakes are important to quick lap times and the Senna could come to a complete stop from 62 mph in less than 100 feet. Each carbon-ceramic brake disc took seven months to create.

The Senna's aggressive styling was an exercise in "form follows function" with an emphasis on generating downforce to keep the car stable at high speeds. McLaren claimed the Senna generated 1763 pounds of downforce at 155 mph.

The cost of the Senna was around $1 million, but the 500-car quota was sold out before production began.